In Tune with the World

In Tune with the World
A Theory of Festivity

Josef Pieper

Translated by Richard and Clara Winston

St. Augustine's Press
South Bend, Indiana

Original German title: *Zustimmung zur Welt: Eine Theorie des Festes*

Manufactured in the United States of America.

4 5 6 7 8   28 27 26 25 24 23 22 21

Library of Congress Cataloging in Publication Data
Pieper, Josef, 1904–1997
    [Zustimmung zur Welt. English]
    In tune with the world : a theory of festivity / Josef
Pieper; translated by Richard and Clara Winston.
        p. cm.
    Includes bibliographical references.
    ISBN 1-890318-33-7 (alk. paper)
    1. Festivals. I. Title.

GT3930.P433 1999   99-14341
394.26—dc21   CIP

The paper used in this publication meets the minimum requirements of the American National Standard for Information Sciences—Permanence of Paper for Printed Materials, ANSI Z39.48-1984.

Acknowledgment is made for permission to use quotations from stanzas VI and VII from "Bread and Wine" in Hölderlin Poems translated by Michael Hamburger, The Harvill Press Ltd., London.

Contents

V

The outward aspect of festivity. Sunday and Easter: the fundamental forms of the Christian holiday. Sabbath and Sunday. The inescapable involvement in theological controversy. The Seventh Day: celebration of the gift of being created and image of the coming age. Easter, "the" festival of the Church. "We have unending holiday."   44

VI

Festivals and the fine arts. Both have an "insular" character. The realization of festivity in the medium of the arts. The place of art is in the festival. Affirmation as the foundation of all arts. "C'est l'amour qui chante." The origin of language in festival. Poésie noire. Pseudo-art and pseudo-festivity. What is a "period of dearth"?   52

VII

Corruption of traditional festivals by commercialism. Artificial holidays established by men. "The day the Lord has made." Festivals of the French Revolution. Direct repression of religious holidays. Coerciveness and manipulated rejoicing. Unreality and boredom. Tragic operetta. The people as object of the celebration. The legislator as a "priest of social felicity."   60

VIII

Historical origin of the socialist May Day celebration. Day of rest and strikes. Rejection of traditional festivals as bourgeois institutions. The first of May under the dictatorship of the proletariat: a "holiday of voluntary work" (Maxim Gorky). Labor army and labor deserters. The crucial factor:

NOTE TO THE READER

The German word *Fest* embraces the meanings of English feast, festival, festivity, fête, holiday, and kindred notions. The German Feier (from Latin *feria*) also has a broad spectrum of meanings: celebration, solemnization, leisure, time after work, holiday, etc. In this translation, no attempt has been made to establish a consistent terminology based on these words; they are rendered differently in different contexts. It may, however, be helpful to the reader to realize that either *Fest* or *Feier*, or its derivatives, underlies the English variants.

In Tune with the World

UBI CARIT AS GAUDET
IBI EST FESTIVIT AS
Chrysostom

I

Certain things can be adequately discussed only if at the same time we speak of the whole of the world and of life. If we are not ready to do that, we give up all claim to saying anything significant. Death and love are such subjects. Festivity, too, must be included in that category. This becomes apparent as soon as we try to get beyond mere description of the facts.

Let us start with what lies nearest to hand. If, for example, we consider the distinction between the festive and the workaday, we soon realize that the antithesis belongs to quite a different category from, say, that of left and right, or day and night. We do not mean only that a working day and a feast day are mutually exclusive; we also mean that work is an everyday occurrence, while a feast is something special, unusual, an interruption in the ordinary passage of time. "A holiday every day" – even every other day – is an idea that cannot be realized in practice; even though it may not necessarily run counter to the concept of festivity in itself,[1] it is hardly feasible in the lives of men existing here and now. The festive quality of a holiday depends on its being exceptional. A

3

festival can arise only out of the foundation of a life whose ordinary shape is given by the working day.

An idle-rich class of do-nothings are hard put to it even to amuse themselves, let alone to celebrate a festival. The *dolce vita* is a desperately unfestive affair. There is, incidentally, considerable testimony that this sad truth applied also to the courtly festivals of the Baroque period, which many an innocent historian has described as highly festive occasions. The probability is that they sprang not from joy in living, but from fear, from *horror vacui*, because the true prerequisite for festivity was lacking at these courts. They had "no everyday life and no work, nothing but time on their hands and boredom."[2]

Incidentally, pseudo-festivals exist, as well as pseudo-work. Not all activity, not every kind of expenditure of effort and earning of money, deserves the name of work. That should be applied only to the active – and usually also laborious – procurement of the things that are truly useful for living. And it is a good guess that only *meaningful* work can provide the soil in which festivity flourishes. Perhaps both work and celebration spring from the same root, so that when the one dries up, the other withers.

But of course meaningful work signifies more than the mere fact of workaday accomplishment. The implication is that man understands the work and accepts it for what it really is, namely, the "tilling of the field" which always includes both happiness and toil, satisfaction as well as sweat of the brow, joy as well as the consumption of vital energy. If one element in these pairs is suppressed, the reality of work is falsified and festivity is ruled out.

We must consider this matter in more concrete terms. In a totalitarian state labor is glorified, and government propaganda romanticizes rises in the production indices as if work were itself a form of celebration. At the same time, true festivity cannot exist in such a state; the very nature of the state is against it. But the possibility or festivity is destroyed even more thoroughly by the other falsification, the view that man's daily life, taken as a whole, is nothing but vexation, meaningless bustle, deadly drudgery, in a word: an absurdity – which, however, the intrepid man who wishes to surrender neither his dignity nor his clarity of vision will not simply endure in dull passivity, but will explicitly affirm and "choose," for the sake of its very absurdity. "One must imagine Sisyphus happy," says Albert Camus.[3] Not that this strenuously pursued happiness, this celebration of the "victory of the absurd," is very credible. In fact it is even less credible than the touted "radiant expression" of the tractor driver who is meeting his quota. Neither the dedication of the Stakhanovite nor the doggedness of Sisyphus allows room for the spontaneity of life which is indispensable to festal exaltation. For that, it is essential to look upon reality whole, and above all "to taste things as they really are,"[4] the bitter bitter and the sweet sweet.

To be sure, bitterness itself can contain a healing element; the good may be found in the bad, *bonum in malo*.[5] This remarkable postulate holds, apparently, only in a single context. I hesitate to call it by name, because to do so will inevitably give rise to a host of misunderstandings, if not worse. I refer to the context of *just punishment*, and to the fact that the soundest, sanest, and most therapeutic thing a justly punished person can do is to accept his punishment as his due, and not try to falsify it by pretending that he enjoys the taste of it, or that he has chosen it. For by enduring the bitterness, the *malum*, he may hope that at least by his own life he is atoning for what he has done, repairing the wrong and turning evil to good; that he is restoring a balance that could not be restored in any other way.

The fact is, as everyone knows, that Christendom's sacred books call work, and incidentally death also, a punishment. That is a subject too broad to discuss here. If we even attempted it, we should have to answer the question: Why has punishment been imposed, and by whom? And then we should find ourselves squarely in the heart of theology. Still, it is good to remind ourselves that such questions can be meaningfully asked, and can also be answered. And it is good for us to be leavened, now and again, by the idea that a path has already been laid down and leads away from an attitude toward work that is essentially inhuman in both its affirmative and negative aspects.

The real nature of festivity, of course, is not made apparent solely by its contrast to labor. A festival is not just a day without work, of course. This must be stated, because some writers have tried to define the essence of festivity only in terms of this difference.[6] Ordinary speech must be taken at its face value, the argument runs; as a rule people can say no more about a successful festival than that it was "something different, for a change," that "you felt as if you were transported to another world for the time being." This, the argument continues, expresses precisely "what makes the celebration a celebration": that "something other ... than daily life ... becomes accessible in it." However, the author adds – he is a theologian – no one is going to be duped into imagining that "either a village shooting contest or, say, a 'festival' play is really 'another world'" – for which reason "the phenomenon of genuine celebration[7] ... is really present only in religious acts in which man as creature can grasp the truly 'other' and absolutely 'new' world of the glory of God." This observation, however, indicates that we need to understand more about the dichotomy between the festive and the everyday than that they are opposites. At one point or another we must define the inner nature of this difference in positive terms.

To do so, we need not immediately cross the border into theological territory, as we have done here – although that border is, of course, not far away. First, it will be profitable to examine somewhat more closely the relationship of festivity to work. In doing so, we find that we can come closer to formulating the quality of a festival, and that it is more than the pause which interrupts the normal course of everyday work. To be sure, it is that too; let us remember that Plato calls the religious holiday a breathing spell,[8] *anápaula*. A day off from work, a day free from the necessity of earning one's livelihood, is after all essential to a festival; in other words, a day free of *servile* work.

Quite understandably, that adjective *servile* brings us up short. Yet concealed behind it is an insight indispensable to our grasping the essence of festivity. It must be noted in passing that the underlying concept of *artes serviles* originally carried no slightest implication of contempt. Rather, the term referred only to activity serving a purpose outside itself (our corresponding adjective would be "useful" or "utilitarian"). But quite aside from the connotation of the term, servile work is by nature dependent on something else. It cannot be thought of apart from its purpose. As a concept, it is part of a system of ideas, and we can scarcely consider it without considering its co-ordinate counterpart.[9] That counterpart is not inactivity or nonwork, but free activity, *ars liberalis*: work that does not have a purpose outside itself, that is meaningful in itself, and for that very reason is neither useful in the strict sense, nor servile or serviceable.

At this point we can grasp the very tip, at least, of that hidden insight. Far be it from us to suggest that activity that is meaningful in itself is synonymous with festivity. But we have, it would seem, discovered a crucial component of festivity. To celebrate a festival means to do something which is in no way tied to other goals, which has been removed from all "so that" and "in order to." True festivity cannot be imagined as residing anywhere but in the realm of activity that is meaningful in itself.

The further implication is, then, that anyone who is at a loss to say what activity that is meaningful in itself is will also be at a loss to define the concept of festivity. And if that incapacity is existential, instead of merely intellectual, then the prerequisite for achieving any kind of festivity is lacking. With the death of the concept of human activity that is meaningful in itself, the possibility of any resistance to a totalitarian laboring society also perishes (and such a regime could very well be established even without concomitant political dictatorship). It then becomes a sheer impossibility to establish and maintain an area of existence which is not preempted by work. For there is only a single justification for not working that will be acceptable even to one's own conscience. That is, dedication of leisure to something meaningful in itself. It is more important not only "socially" but also on a higher human level to work than to kill time; and if we contrast the laboring society and its totalitarian planning for utility with a civilization dedicated mainly to entertainment, the former seems without question overwhelmingly superior.

Incidentally, we may have reached a point when the practical prerequisite to festivity, liberation from work, is itself becoming a dubious proposition. It was recently pointed out, with the utmost seriousness, that the age-old human dream of a life free of toil is on the verge of being uncannily fulfilled and, "like the fulfillment of wishes in fairy-tales, comes at a moment when it can only be self-defeating" because the "laboring society" no longer knows "of those other and more meaningful activities for the sake of which this freedom would deserve to be won."[10]

How can we visualize something that serves nothing else, that by its very nature has meaning only in its own terms?

Almost inevitably there comes to mind a notion that has been much discussed in anthropological literature of recent decades – although it has been the subject of considerable romantic speculation, as well as of sound analysis. I am referring to the concept of *play*. Does not play epitomize that pure purposefulness in itself, we might ask? Is not play activity meaningful in itself, needing no utilitarian justification? And should not festivity therefore be interpreted chiefly as a form of play?

Obviously, these are extremely complex questions which cannot be settled merely in passing. Nevertheless, we would hazard that the term *play* does not adequately define the distinguishing feature of free activity, let alone of festivity. To be sure, Plato closely associates the two ideas when he speaks of "the graciousness of play and festival."[11] And if "seriousness," as Hegel says, "is work in relation to the need,"[12] then it does seem logical to equate play with festivity in similar fashion. In fact a real festival can scarcely be conceived unless the ingredient of play – perhaps also, although here I am not so sure, the ingredient of playfulness – has entered into it. But all this has not answered the crucial question of whether the element of play makes an action meaningful in itself. Human acts derive their meaning primarily from their content, from their object, not from the manner in which they are performed. Play, however, seems to be chiefly a mere *modus* of action, a specific way of performing something, at any rate a purely formal determinant. Thus it is natural enough that people inevitably flounder in phantasms and unrealities when they try to regard all those human activities that are obviously not just work as play and nothing more: the work of the artist, too – of the writer, musician, painter – or even religious worship. For suddenly everything that was "meaningful in itself" slips through their fingers and becomes a game empty of all meaning. Significantly, one good argument against Huizinga's book on *homo ludens*, which represents the religious festivals of primitive peoples purely as play,[13] is that this view is tantamount to saying that all sacred acts are meaningless. Incidentally, this objection has not been made by a theologian; the critic is an ethnologist, protesting against distortion of empirical observation.[14]

The question, then, remains open: By what virtue does an act possess the inner quality of being meaningful in itself?

II

But, someone may remonstrate, "does not everyone know what a festival is, anyhow?" The question is not altogether irrelevant. However, "If no one asks me, I know: if I wish to explain it to one that asks, I know not." This sentence from St. Augustine's *Confessions*.[1] although written in relation to something else, is highly applicable to the concept of festivity. The problem is to put into words what everyone means and knows.

Nowadays, however, we are forcefully "asked" both what a festival is and, even more, what the psychological prerequisites are for celebrating one. "The trick is not to arrange a festival, but to find people who can *enjoy* it." The man who jotted down this aphorism nearly one hundred years ago was Friedrich Nietzsche;[2] his genius, as this sentence once again illustrates, lay to no small degree in that seismographic sensitivity to what was to come. The implication is that festivity in general is in danger of extinction, for arrangements alone do not make a festival. Since Nietzsche's day it has become a more or less standard matter to connect the "misery of this present age" with "man's incapacity for festivity."[3] We may, of course, suspect that this gloomy diagnosis rather oversimplifies. In all ages, the chances are, it was never easy to meet the requirement that great festivals be celebrated in the proper spirit. As the history of religions tells us,[4] empty and wearisome pomp existed even at the Greek festivals. Nevertheless, it is peculiar to our time that we may conceive of festivity itself as being expressly repudiated. This very situation gives rise to the "question," prompts us to decide for ourselves what presumably everybody knows and takes for granted: namely, what the essence of festivity is, and what should be done so that men in our time can preserve or regain the capacity to celebrate real festivals festively – a capacity which concerns the heart of life, and perhaps constitutes it. Mere description of classical or medieval or even East Indian festivals, no matter how accurate and stirring, does not further our aim at all. Even a "morphology," stylistic history, or sociology of festivals would not especially help us.[5] Such studies not only rail to answer the question; they do not even touch it. We must attack the question in a far more fundamental sense.

But does not celebrating a festival mean simply the equivalent of having a good time? And does not everyone know what that is? Perhaps so – but again a few questions arise. What *is* a good time? Does anything of the sort exist? May it not be that the only kind of good time that is really possible is a time of good work?

These are questions we cannot answer unless we have a conception of man. For what is involved is the fulfillment of human life, and the form in which this fulfillment is to take place. Inevitably, therefore, we find ourselves concerned with such ideas as "the perfection of man," "eternal life," "bliss," "Paradise." Now, there is little point in learning what any individual thinks all on his own about such fundamental matters, no matter how original his ideas may be. In this realm, we should be wary of originality. It is more rewarding to consider what the tradition of humanity's wisdom, into which the thought of whole generations has entered, has to tell us. To be sure, we need scarcely expect that this tale will be easy to decipher.

The traditional name for the utmost perfection to which man may attain, the fulfillment of his being, is *visio beatifica*, the "seeing that confers bliss." This is to say that the highest intensification of life, the absolutely perfect activity, the final stilling of all volition, and the partaking of the utmost fullness that life can offer, takes place as a kind of seeing; more precisely, that all this is achieved in seeing awareness of the divine ground of the universe.[6]

Incidentally, the tradition in which this view may be found extends much further back than the Christian centuries, perhaps back beyond historical time altogether. A few generations before Plato, the Greek Anaxagoras, in answer to the question of what he had been bom for, replied: "For seeing." And in Plato's *Symposium* Diotima clearly expresses the traditional wisdom of the *visio beatified*: "This is that life above all others which man should live, in the contemplation of divine beauty; this makes man immortal."[7]

But eschatology alone is not the issue; the traditional wisdom does not speak only of the ultimate perfection of life in the hereafter." It speaks also of man as an earthly being appearing in history, and asserts that man by nature craves the appeasement of his yearnings through seeing. In this present life also, the utmost happiness takes the form of contemplation.[8] "Most of all we esteem the sense of sight," Aristotle says in the very beginning of his *Metaphysics*. And Pierre Teilhard de Chardin belongs to the same tradition when he suggests (in the remarkable chapter on vision which surprisingly opens his book, *The Phenomenon of Man*) that all life is comprehended within seeing, and that the whole evolution of the cosmos aims above all at "the elaboration of ever more perfect eyes."[9]

Such "earthly" contemplation can take a good many different forms. It may be the philosopher's consideration of the Whole of existence; or the particular vision of the artist, who seeks to penetrate to the prototypal images of things in the universe; or the contemplative prayer of one absorbed in the divine mysteries. Whenever anyone succeeds in bringing before his mind's eye the hidden ground of everything that is, he succeeds to the same degree in performing an act that is meaningful in itself, and has a "good time."

From this it follows that the concept of festivity is inconceivable without an element of contemplation. This does not mean exerting the argumentative intellect, but the "simple intuition" of reason; not the unrest of thought, but the mind's eye resting on whatever manifests itself. It means a relaxing of the strenuous fixation of the eye on the given frame of reference, without which no utilitarian act is accomplished. Instead, the field of vision widens, concern for success or failure of an act falls away, and the soul turns to its infinite object; it becomes aware of the illimitable horizon of reality as a whole.

Ethnological and historico-cultural writers have often pointed out that "a union of peace, intensity of life, and contemplation"[10] is essential for festivity, so that to celebrate a festival is equivalent to "becoming contemplative and, in this state, directly confronting the higher realities on which the whole of existence rests."[11] Such observations accord completely with everyone's experience. Bustle does not make a festival; on the contrary, it can spoil one. Of course this does not mean that a festival is simply contemplation and recollection of self; any such claim is clearly belied by experience. Nevertheless, we cling to the feeling that a special spice, essential to the right celebration of a festival, is a kind of expectant alertness. One must be able to look through and, as it were, beyond the immediate matter of the festival, including the festal gifts; one must engage in a listening, and therefore necessarily silent, meditation upon the fundament of existence. The only truly legitimate reason for a day free from work is this form of recognition of what is meaningful in itself. In a work written by Thomas Aquinas[12] in his youth this idea is expressed in an unusual way. He comments that the Roman philosopher Seneca was not so wrong in his mockery of the Jewish Sabbath for being filled with empty rituals. For, he says, such a day is not lost, *non amittitur*, only "if that is done on the Sabbath for which it is appointed: the contemplation of divine things," *divinorum contemplatio*.

The antithesis between holiday and workday, or more precisely, the concept of the day of rest, tells us something further about the essence of festivity. The day of rest is not just a neutral interval inserted as a link in the chain of workaday life. It entails a loss of utilitarian profit. In voluntarily keeping the holiday, men renounce the yield of a day's labor. This renunciation has from time immemorial been regarded as an essential element of festivity.[13] A definite span of usable time is made, as the ancient Romans understood it, "the exclusive property of the gods."[14] As the animal for sacrifice was taken from the herd, so a piece of available time was expressly withdrawn from utility.[15] The day of rest, then, meant not only that no work was done, but also that an offering was being made of the yield of labor. It is not merely that the time is not gainfully used; the offering is in the nature of a sacrifice, and therefore the diametric opposite of utility.

It scarcely need be said that in a world governed by the concept of utility, there can be no time set aside on principle, any more than there can be land set aside on principle. Anyone' who called for it would be accused of "sabotaging work." For that very reason the totalitarian laboring society must of necessity be an altogether unfestive society, just as it is marked by scarcity and impoverishment even when there is the greatest abundance of material goods. Similarly, the man who is limited to absolutely utilitarian activity, to the *artes serviles*, and who is thus "proletarianized" in that sense, has rightly been called "unfestive."[16] On the other hand, voluntary renunciation of the yield of a working day cuts through the principle of calculating utility, and the principle of poverty also. Even in conditions of extreme material scarcity, the withholding from work, in the midst of a life normally governed by work, creates an area of free surplus.

This, then, unexpectedly brings us to a new aspect of a holiday. A festival is essentially a phenomenon of wealth; not, to be sure, the wealth of money, but of existential richness. Absence of calculation, in fact lavishness, is one of its elements. Of course there is a natural peril and a germ of degeneration inherent in this. The way is open to senseless and excessive waste of the yield of work, to an extravagance that violates all rationality. The product of a whole year's labor can be thrown away on a single day. As is well known, men are quite capable of such behavior. But this potential perversion cannot be included within the definition of festivity, as has recently been done.[17] We may properly say that every festival conceals within itself "at least a germ of excess";[18] but it is highly misleading if festival itself is defined as "le paroxysme de la société,"[19] as a submergence in "creative" chaos. True enough, the fact remains that the paramountcy of a calculating, economizing mentality prevents both festive excess and festivity itself. In the workaday world all magnificence and pomp is calculated, and therefore unfestive. The myriad lights of a commercialized Christmas inevitably seem basically meager, without any real radiance. We remember G. K. Chesterton's keen comment on the dazzling advertisements of Times Square at night: What a glorious sight for those who luckily do not know how to read.

Such an act of renunciation and sacrificial offering, however, cannot be imagined as being performed at random. The talk of "valuable working time" is, after all, not just talk; something utterly real is involved. Why should anyone decide to sacrifice this precious article without sufficient reason? If we probe a little more insistently for a reason, we find a curious analogy to the other, the contemplative aspect of the day of rest, of which we have already spoken. The achievement of contemplation, since it is the seeing, the intuition of the beloved object,[20] presupposes a specific non-intellectual, direct, and existential relation to reality, an existential concord of man with the world and with himself. Precisely in the same way, the act of freely giving oneself cannot take place unless it likewise grows from the root of a comprehensive affirmation – for which no other term can be found than "love." In spite of the thickets of banality, sentimentality, and unrealistic spiritualization that threaten to smother the true meaning of this word, it remains indispensable. There is no other word that so precisely denotes what is at issue.

We do not renounce things, then, except for love. This hypothesis will have to be examined more closely. Nevertheless, we have not advanced it without considerable thought. Above all, we hope that it will serve as a new vantage point from which we will be able to see more deeply into the idea as well as the actuality of festivity.

III

Perhaps because we are so allergic to big words, we hesitate to speak of a festival as a "day of rejoicing." All the same, we should have to concur if someone chose to understate a little and called it at the least a "joyous affair." On a festival day, people enjoy themselves. Even one who terms it quite a "trick" to find such people is merely saying that it has become difficult and rare to celebrate a festival festively. But no one denies that it should be, by its nature, a day of rejoicing. An early Christian Greek went so far as to say: "Festivity is joy and nothing else."[1]

Now it is the nature of joy to be a secondary phenomenon. No one can rejoice "absolutely," for joy's sake alone. To be sure, it is foolish to ask a man why he wants to rejoice – to that extent joy is an end in itself. Nevertheless, the longing for joy is nothing but the desire to have a reason and pretext for joy. This reason, to the extent that it actually exists, precedes joy and is different from it. The reason comes first; the joy comes second.

But the reason for joy, although it may be encountered in a thousand concrete forms, is always

In Tune with the World

the same: possessing or receiving what one loves, whether actually in the present, hoped for in the future, or remembered in the past.[2] Joy is an expression of love. One who loves nothing and nobody cannot possibly rejoice, no matter how desperately he craves joy. Joy is the response of a lover receiving what he loves.

True as it is that a real festival cannot be conceived without joy, it is no less true that first there must be a substantial reason for joy, which might also be called the festive occasion. Strictly speaking, it is not enough for this reason to exist objectively. Men must also accept and acknowledge it as a reason for joy; they must experience it themselves as a receiving of something they love. An odd sort of objectivity has sometimes been attributed to festivals, as though they could exist even without people: "It is . . . Easter even where nobody celebrates it."[3] It seems to me that such a notion is illusory, as long as we are speaking of festivals as a human reality.

The inner structure of real festivity has been stated in the clearest and tersest possible fashion by Chrysostom: *Ubi caritas gaudet, ibi est festivitas,*[4] "Where love rejoices, there is festivity."

Now, what sort of reason underlies festal joy and therefore festivity itself? "Plant a flower-decked pole in the middle of an open place, call the people together – and you have a fête!" Everyone – one would think – sees that that is not enough. But I did not invent the sentence as an

23

example of naïve simplification. It was written by
Jean Jacques Rousseau.[5]

It is an almost equally hopeless simplification
to imagine that mere ideas can be the occasion for
real festivals. Something more is needed, something of another order. The celebrant himself must
have shared in a distinctly real experience. When
Easter is declared a festival of "immortality," it is
scarcely surprising that no response is forthcom-
ing – not to speak of such fantastic proposals as
those of Auguste Comte, whose reformed calendar established festivals of Humanity, Paternity,
and even Domesticity. Not even the idea of freedom can inspire people with a spirit of festivity,
though the celebration of liberation might – assuming that the event though possibly belonging
to the distant past, still has compelling contemporary force. Memorial days are not in themselves
festival days. Strictly speaking, the past cannot be
celebrated festively unless the celebrant community still draws glory and exaltation from that
past, not merely as reflected history, but by virtue
of a historical reality still operative in the present.[6]
If the Incarnation of God is no longer understood
as an event that directly concerns the present lives
of men, it becomes impossible, even absurd, to
celebrate Christmas festively.

Josef Andreas Jungmann has recently suggested that festivals as an institution have already
become derivative, whereas the "prototypal form"
of festival still takes place where a specific event

such as birth, marriage, or homecoming is being directly celebrated.[7] If the implication is that the specific event is the real reason of all celebrations, and also the highest rationale which a modern theory of festivals can provide, the thesis is not altogether convincing. We can and must pursue the inquiry further, to ask, for example: On what grounds does a specific event become the occasion for festival and celebration? Can we festively celebrate the birth of a child if we hold with Jean Paul Sartre's dictum: "It is absurd that we are bom"?[8] Anyone who is seriously convinced that "our whole existence is something that would be better not being,"[9] and that consequently life is not worth living, can no wore celebrate the birth of his child than any other birthday, his own or anyone else's, a fiftieth or sixtieth or any other. No single specific event can become the occasion for festive celebrations unless – unless what?

Here is where we must be able to name the reason underlying all others, the "reason why" events such as birth, marriage, homecoming are felt as the receiving of something beloved, without which there can be neither joy nor festivity. Again we find Nietzsche expressing the crucial insight – one painfully brought home, it would seem, as the result of terrible inner trials, for he was as familiar with the despair of being unable to take "enough joy in anything"[10] as with "the vast unbounded Yea- and Amen-saying."[11] The formulation is to be found in his posthumous notes, and reads: "To have joy in anything, one must approve everything."[12]

Underlying all festive joy kindled by a specific circumstance there has to be an absolutely universal affirmation extending to the world as a whole, to the reality of things and the existence of man himself. Naturally, this approval need not be a product of conscious reflection; it need not be formulated at all. Nevertheless, it remains the sole foundation for festivity, no matter what happens to be celebrated *in concreto*. And as the radical nature of negation deepens, and consequently as anything but ultimate arguments becomes ineffectual, it becomes more necessary to refer to this ultimate foundation. By ultimate foundation I mean the conviction that the prime festive occasion, which alone can ultimately justify all celebration, really exists; that, to reduce it to the most concise phrase, at bottom *everything that is, is good, and it is good to exist*. For man cannot have the experience of receiving what is loved, unless the world and existence as a whole represent something good and therefore beloved to him.

Incidentally, there is a kind of confirmation of this from the other shore, as it were. Whenever we happen to feel heartfelt assent, to find that something specific is good, wonderful, glorious, rapturous – a drink of fresh water, the precise functioning of a tool, the colors of a landscape, the charm of a loving gesture, a poem – our praise always reaches beyond the given object, if matters take their natural course. Our tribute always contains at least a smattering of affirmation of the world, as a whole. So that the converse of the sentence we have just quoted is also valid – and again Nietzsche has formulated it: "If it be granted that we say Yea to a single moment, then in so doing we have said Yea not only to ourselves, but to all existence."[13]

Need we bother to say how little such affirmation has to do with shallow optimism, let alone with smug approval of that which is? Such affirmation is not won by deliberately shutting one's eyes to the horrors in this world. Rather, it proves its seriousness by its confrontation with historical evil. The quality of this assent is such that we must attribute it even to martyrs, at the very moment, perhaps, that they perish under brutal assault. A theologian commenting on the Apocalypse has said[14] that what distinguishes the Christian martyr is that he never utters a word against God's Creation. In spite of everything he finds the things that are "very good"; therefore in spite of everything he remains capable of joy and even, as far as it concerns him, of festivity. Whereas, on the other hand, whoever refuses assent to reality as a whole, no matter how well off he may be, is by that fact incapacitated for either joy or festivity. Festivity is impossible to the naysayer. The more money he has, and above all the more leisure, the more desperate is this impossibility to him.

This is also true of the man who refuses to approve the fact of his own existence – having fallen into that mysterious, ineffable "despair from weakness" of which Sören Kierkegaard[15] has spoken and which in the old moral philosophy went by the name of *acedia*, "slothfulness of the heart."[16] At issue is a refusal regarding the very heart and fountainhead of existence itself, because of the "despair of not willing to be oneself"[17] which makes man unable to live with himself. He is driven out of his own house – into the hurly-burly of work-and-nothing-else, into the fine-spun exhausting game of sophistical phrase-mongering, into incessant "entertainment" by empty stimulants – in short, into a no man's land which may be quite comfortably furnished, but which has no place for the serenity of intrinsically meaningful activity, for contemplation, and certainly not for festivity.

Festivity lives on affirmation. Even celebrations for the dead, All Souls and Good Friday, can never be truly celebrated except on the basis of faith that all is well with the world and life as a whole. If there is no consolation, the idea of a funeral as a solemn act is self-contradictory. But consolation is a form of rejoicing, although the most silent of all – just as catharsis, the purification of the soul in the witnessing of tragedy, is at bottom a *joyful* experience. (The real locus of the tragic is not in those works of literature we term tragedies, but in man's historical reality.) Consolation exists only on the premise that grief, sorrow, death, are accepted, and therefore affirmed, as meaningful in spite of everything.

This is the point at which to correct the misconception which sometimes prevails,[18] that the festive is also the cheerful. It is significant that according to Greek myth all great festivals had their origins in the celebration of funeral rites.[19] And historians of religion have repeatedly pointed out that the ancient Roman festivals must not be considered simply as days of rejoicing.[20] Naturally, for a festival to develop a broad and rich appeal, jesting, gaiety, and laughter cannot be excluded from it, nor even some riotousness and carnival. But a festival becomes true festivity only when man affirms the goodness of his existence by offering the response of joy. Can it be that this goodness is never revealed to us so brightly and powerfully as by the sudden shock of loss and death? This is the implication of Holderlin's famous distich (on Sophocles' *Antigone*):

Viele versuchten umsonst, das Freudigste freudig zu sagen,
   Hier spricht endlich es mir, hier in der Trauer sich aus.

Many endeavored in vain joyfully to speak profoundest joy;
   Here at last, in the tragic, I see it expressed.[21]

Is it therefore so surprising that both the affirmation of life and its rejection should be hard to recognize, not only to the eye of the outsider but possibly to one's own inner eye?[22] When we look at the martyr, it is by no means plain that he is affirming the world in spite of everything; for after all, he is not instantly recognizable as a "martyr," but as a defendant, a convict, a ridiculous eccentric – but above all as one who has been silenced. Similarly, non-assent may also appear under a disguise. For example, it may be covered over by pleasure – agreeable enough in itself and springing from sheer vitality – in dancing, music, drinking, so that the rejection remains for a while hidden even from the self. Above all, this rejection may be concealed behind the façade of a more or less sham confidence in life. The jovial laughter of Sisyphus, "who negates the gods and raises rocks,"[23] is deceptive, even in the sense that the deception may succeed or, which would be infinitely harder, that he may deceive himself.

Strictly speaking, however, it is insufficient to call affirmation of the world a mere prerequisite and premise for festivity. In fact it is far more; it is the substance of festivity. Festivity, in its essential core, is nothing but the living out of this affirmation.

To celebrate a festival means to live out, for some special occasion and in an uncommon manner, the universal assent to the world as a whole.

This statement harmonizes with the conclusions cultural and religious historians have drawn from their studies of the great typical festivals in ancient cultures and among primitive peoples. And because that assent to life, if it is there at all, is there all the time, it becomes the wellspring for a thousand legitimate occasions for festivity. The immediate event may be equally the coming of spring or of a baby's first tooth. Consequently, we may properly speak of everlasting festival as existing at least in latent form. In fact, Church liturgy recognizes only festival days – which by a strange and devious linguistic evolution has led to a change in the meaning of *feria*; originally, the word meant "festival," but now it is beginning to signify the festival celebrated on ordinary weekdays.[24] So significant a philosopher and theologian as Origen contended that the naming of specific holy days was done only for the sake of the "uninitiate" and "beginners" who were not yet capable of celebrating the "eternal festival."[25] But it is still too early in our discussion to examine this phase of the matter.

First of all, we must now state explicitly a conclusion toward which all our foregoing ideas have inexorably led. To be sure, as I have found time and again, this statement is usually greeted with alarm and distrust, as though to voice it is somehow equivalent to launching an unfair surprise attack. Nevertheless, I see no legitimate way of avoiding it; it is absolutely compelling, both logically and existentially.

The conclusion is divisible into several parts. *First*: there can be no more radical assent to the world than the praise of God, the lauding of the Creator of this same world. One cannot conceive a more intense, more unconditional affirmation of being. If the heart of festivity consists in men's physically expressing their agreement with everything that is, then – *secondly* – the ritual festival is the most festive form that festivity can possibly take. The other side of this coin is that – *thirdly* – there can be no deadlier, more ruthless destruction of festivity than refusal of ritual praise. Any such Nay tramples out the spark from which the flickering flame of festivity might have been kindled anew.

IV

When we say that the ritual festival is the most festive form of festivity, do we mean that there can be no secular festivals? Of course not. But the matter is complicated, and a simple answer does not suffice.

On the one hand, real festivity cannot be restricted to any one particular sphere of life, neither to the religious nor to any other; it seizes and permeates all dimensions of existence – so that from a mere description of the proceedings we cannot easily tell whether a festival is "really" a social, economic, athletic, or church event, a fair, a dance, or a feast. Until I was eight years old I thought that Whitsun simply meant country fair, because our village would "celebrate" both the same day. In Toledo on Corpus Christi Day the streets, canopied with canvas, are transformed into a vast festive tent whose walls are formed by the tapestry-decked façades of the houses and whose floor is strewn with rosemary and lavender, which give out a stronger perfume the more they are walked on. High Mass in the Cathedral is followed by the procession: a musical performance, military parade, social display, and Exposition of the Sacrament. The bullfight in the afternoon is, of course, as secular as it is at other times; but it is the *Corrida del Corpus*. Wherever festivity can freely vent itself in all its possible forms, an event is produced that leaves no zone of life, worldly or spiritual, untouched.

But now we must consider the "on the other hand." There are worldly, but there are no purely profane, festivals. And we may presume that not only can we not find them, but that they cannot exist. A festival without gods is a non-concept, is inconceivable. For example, Carnival remains festive only where Ash Wednesday still exists. To eliminate Ash Wednesday is to eliminate the Carnival itself. Yet Ash Wednesday is obviously a day in Christendom's liturgical year. The pallor of the merely "legal" holidays is evident from the fact that there is much discussion of how they really should be "celebrated." This is not to say that we should not single out days of "Unity" and "Constitution" and pay them special heed. But can we seriously call them *festival days*? If there were no other evidence against their being festivals, their origin alone would serve. Where in the world has there been a real festival arising from a mere act of legislation, a decision by a representative assembly? Who is empowered to establish a festival? Plato maintained that the "recreation"[1] of festivals was established divinely. And certainly no Christian would say otherwise of the great holy days of Christendom.

Festivals are, it would seem, traditional in a very special sense, a *traditum* in the strictest meaning of that concept: received from a superhuman source, to be handed on undiminished, received and handed on again.[2] It has been said that the living force of tradition is nowhere manifested so clearly as in the history of festivals.[3] That is true. Nevertheless, we must quickly add that the subject entails a whole complex of problems. Real handing down, the living process of transmission from one generation to another, is deterred rather than abetted by the kind of traditionalism that clings to external appearances. For what really matters is not mere preservation and conservation, but a constant succession of new, creative reshapings which give contemporaneity to the content of the festivals. On the other hand, although people are sometimes too ready to talk of breaches of tradition and lack of tradition, such criticism is sometimes quite apt in connection with the decadence of festivals. If the sons truly no longer knew the significance of the great holidays celebrated by their fathers, then the most immediate tie between the generations would be cut and tradition would, strictly speaking, no longer exist.

Secular as well as religious festivals have their roots in the rituals of worship. Otherwise, what arises is not a profane festival, but something quite artificial, which is either an embarrassment or – we shall have more to say on this – a new and more strenuous kind of work.

Side by side with the history of festivals runs the history of their interpretations, thus corroborating the close link between festival and worship in men's thinking. The list of concepts which was long believed to be a work of Plato's, and which is still included in his collected works under the title of *Definitions*,[4] contains a terse phrase for festival: *hierós chrónos*,[5] "holy time." That definition was fully accepted by Cicero[6] and by the people of ancient Rome in general. They regarded a festival as a holy day, *par définition un "jour divin."*[7] The phrase defines the essential trait of festivals, and to the present day that concept holds, however little the question is regarded from a theological point of view. Even in Roger Caillois, one of the few contemporary writers who have attempted a culturo-philosophical theory of festivity, we find the statement that a festival is *"la période de la prééminence du sacré."*[8]

The special relationship of festivals to ritual sacrifices was also recognized and stated very early in the history of our culture. Plato seemed to consider the terms for both as virtually equivalent.[9] And from the time of Augustus, an etymology has come down to us claiming that the very word *feria* derives from the killing of animals for sacrifice, *"a feriendis victimis."*[10] The etymology is wrong, of course; but it proves how unquestioningly these two concepts were considered to be in closest relation to each other. By the same reasoning, the early Christians called exclusion from communion banishment to unfestivity.[11] "The sacrifice is the soul of festivals."[12]

Ritual worship is essentially an expression of the same affirmation that lies at the heart of festivals. Hegel said that the "general character" of Greek worship was "that the subject has an essentially affirmative relationship to his god."[13] This is true not only of the forms of worship practiced in classical antiquity. All worship is affirmation, not only of God but also of the world. Nietzsche, as we know, thought otherwise. When he hailed pagan worship as "a form of affirmation of life,"[14] he was opposing it to Christianity, which he was indicting on that score as well. Along with so much else, the Church had "spoiled" festivals.[15] Of course there are facts that make such charges comprehensible – but no truer. However, that is a separate subject. On the crucial point, at any rate, Nietzsche is perfectly right: festivals are doomed unless they are preceded by the pattern of ritual religious praise. That is the fire that kindles them. But it is that very thing – praise of God – which constitutes almost the entire content of Christian ritual – virtually the only ritual, incidentally, which continues to have meaning within those civilizations that stem from Europe.

We need only examine the liturgical texts for their manifest and overt meaning to see at once, without need for further glosses, that affirmation is the fundamental form of Christian liturgy. Christian liturgy is in fact "an unbounded Yea-and

Amen-saying." Every prayer closes with the word: Amen, thus it is good, thus shall it be, *ainsi soit-il*. What is the *Alleluia* but a cry of jubilation? The heavenly adoration in the Apocalyptic vision[16] is also a single great acclamation, composed of reiterated exclamations of Hail, Praise, Glory, Thanks. St. Augustine has defined worship in the same terms: "Worship takes place," he says,[17] "by the offering of praise and thanksgiving." Indeed, the Church itself uses the name "thanksgiving" for the sacramental offering which is the source and center of all other acts of worship. The Mass is called and is *eucharistia*. Whatever the specific content of this thanksgiving may be, the "occasion" for which it is performed and which it comports with is nothing other than the salvation of the world and of life as a whole. Even the non-Christian, I think, can be asked to take note of this. Of course, everything depends on whether or not we think the historical world and human life are "made whole" or at any rate "capable of being made whole" by Christ. This is the all-important question. I am not actually discussing this question in this book; rather, it is the underlying assumption. My purpose is only to make clear that Christian worship sees itself as an act of affirmation that expresses itself in praise, glorification, thanksgiving for the whole of reality and existence.

The Christian *eucharistia* manifests that in all acts of public worship something else occurs besides the praise or sacrifice performed by human beings. Perhaps it is not quite accurate to say that this something else simply "occurs"; but at any rate, that "occurrence' is always what public worship aims at and hopes for. In practicing the rites of worship men hope that they will be vouchsafed a share in the superhuman abundance of life. From time immemorial, this very thing has always been considered the true, the immanent fruit of all great festivals.

Language harbors a variety of names for this phenomenon: renewal, transformation, restoration, rejuvenation, rebirth. But they all mean the same thing, even though it does not lend itself to clear definition and description. There are many ways in which the gift is experienced. It is recreation; it is, as Goethe put it, release from the pressure of daily obligation. Passing time stands still.[18] The constant attrition of our portion of vital substance is suspended for a moment by that "resting Now" in which the reality of Eternity is revealed. Men are swept away from the here and now to utterly tranquil contemplation of the ground of existence; to happiness, as in absorption in beloved eyes. Everyday things unexpectedly take on the freshness of Eden; the world, again in Goethe's words, is "glorious as on the first of days."[19]

The train of images is endless. But all of them convey the same meaning: that the fruit of the festival, for which alone it is really celebrated, is pure gift; it is the element of festivity that can never be "organized," arranged and induced. The will is bent on action; however easy it may seem, we have far less talent for relaxation, slackening effort, letting ourselves go, than for the hard task of work. To be sure, relaxation can be learned and practiced to a certain degree. But no amount of effort, no matter how desperate, can force festivity to yield up its essence. All we can do is prepare ourselves to receive the hoped-for gift; and perhaps the idea of "ritual purity," which as has been said is inherent in the idea of festivity,[20] should be rethought and recaptured. All these considerations, however, do not in any way nullify the nature of the gift, which is in no way pledged, predictable, or meritable, and descends only of its own accord. "In order for a festival to emerge out of human efforts, something divine must be added, which alone makes possible the otherwise impossible."[21] That is an ethnologist's conclusion, but it applies not only to primitive peoples. It suddenly makes us realize the very real sense of the statement in both the Psalms[22] and the Platonic Dialogue[23] that the festival is a day God has made.

Thus, when a festival goes as it should, men receive something that it is not in human power to give. This is the by now almost forgotten reason for the age-old custom of men wishing one another well on great festival days. What are we really wishing our fellow men when we send them "best wishes for Christmas"? Health, enjoyment of each other's company, thriving children, success – all these things, too, of course. We may even – why not? – be wishing them a good appetite for the holiday meal. But the real thing we are wishing is the "success" of the festive celebration itself, not just its outer forms and enrichments, not the trimmings, but the gift that is meant to be the true fruit of the festival: renewal, transformation, rebirth. Nowadays, to be sure, all this can barely be sensed behind the trite formula: "Happy holidays."

"Swept away from the here and now." That phrase, which we used above, merits brief consideration. If it is not just a poetic exaggeration – and it is not meant as such – it suggests among other things that a "there and then" exists. It suggests also that the true existence of man takes place in both spheres. Nor is there very much theology underlying this idea. It is merely the simple conclusion to be drawn from the creatureliness of reality. In regarding man and world as *creatura* we imply that our own existence, as well as that of things, is founded upon the non-temporal, non-successive, and therefore still continuing act of creation. Existence as we know it, therefore, does not just "adjoin" the realm of Eternity; it is entirely permeated by it. Not that we can, by our power and volition, "step out of time." Nevertheless, to do so remains among our real potentialities. And these potentialities are realized in the rapture of the true celebrant. Suddenly the walls of the solid here and now are burst asunder and the everyday realm of existence is thrown open to Eternity.[24] "To celebrate a festival means to enter into the presence of the Deity."[25]

Of course rapture is always a shattering of man's ordinary, "normal" relationship to the world. And as in the case of the shattering emotions of erotic or artistic experience,[26] which threaten to overwhelm the rational order of existence, festivals naturally carry with them the danger of both interrupting the orderly course of human events and opening them to question. We have already spoken of that.

A true festival does not take place "here" at all. It "occurs only apparently here and now... not in time, but beyond time." This sentence from a modern philosophical essay[27] on culture might be concluded by a quotation from Origen's commentary on John,[28] without creating a feeling of discrepancy: "... not in this eon nor on earth." History seems to agree. As Wilamowitz tells us,[29] one of the great Attic festivals, the Cronia, came about so that "men might taste for a single day the blessed life enjoyed in the Golden Age under Cronos." It hardly matters whether we conceive of festivals as anchored in the extrahistorical past or the extrahistorical future: The concept of *paradiso* includes both dimensions. When, therefore, Roger Caillois speaks of the recall of the primordial, mythic past and of the festival as *"une actualisation des premiers temps de l'univers,"*[30] he is not very far from what the Greek theologian Athanasius said in the fourth century: "To us who live here our festivals are an

42

unobstructed passage to that life."[31] The common meaning of all these statements is clear: In celebrating festivals festively, man passes beyond the barriers of this present life on earth.

Inability to be festive, on the other hand, can be explained in such a way as to illuminate the core of the problem. It signifies "immurement" within the zone of the given present, "exposure to the tenors of history."[32] Festivity, on the other hand, is a liberation. Through it the celebrant becomes aware of, and may enter, the greater reality which gives a wider perspective on the world of everyday work, even as it supports it.

V

In spite of cultural history and modern ethnology, we know little about the inner nature of the hunting and harvest festivals of savages, the Eleusinian festival of the Greeks or the secular festivals of Augustan Rome. And today, even when we attend the religious festivals of alien cultures, we can scarcely deceive ourselves into thinking we understand them. At bottom, we must admit, they remain inaccessible to us. This does not mean that sociological data and statistics can tell us nothing about festivals. After all, festivals are public by nature; they are affairs of the community, in fact its "self-portrait,"[1] and consequently visible, "objective" events. An instructive way to begin such an inquiry might be to see how a red-letter day in the calendar differs from other days of the year. Incidentally, in approaching the problem in this factual way, we cannot fail to notice that here and there a day that is still called a holiday is no longer celebrated as such. We may next notice that there are so-called days of rest, designated as such by law and governed by law. (Ancient Rome, by the way, agreed with Old Testament Judaism on the principle underlying such regulations. In the

Georgics[2] Virgil lists the activities permitted to peasants on holidays. The famous formula that everything is permitted that it would be injurious to omit, *quod praetermissum noceret*, was first handed down by the ancient Roman jurist Scaevola.[3])

Nevertheless, the fact remains that what really happens in the celebration of a festival cannot be identified immediately from outward appearances. For true understanding, it is necessary to enter a chamber that is barred to non-initiates. Thus the only festivals whose invisible core we can directly comprehend are the Christian holidays. At first sight there seem to be a multitude of them, but they reduce down to two: Sunday and Easter. Josef Andreas Jungmann has recently set forth that idea in a wholly convincing way. His conclusion is: "To read the original idea of the Christian festival, we must look to Sunday and to Easter."[4]

If Sunday is no more than a day free of work, established by men for purely practical reasons and therefore also a convenient time for common religious services; if it is really "nothing but a voluntary institution of the community" and distinctly "not divinely founded" – then the quality of a holy day can scarcely be attributed to it. That, I think, should be clear even before we begin studying the nature of Sunday in detail. This is the view taken by the theologian Gunther Dehn[5] in the *Evangelisches Soziallexikon* (1954). We can understand it only if we consider it in conjunction with another, equally theological argument. For the same author takes up the question of whether the Christian Sunday is related to the Old Testament Sabbath, in which case what the Holy Scriptures have to say about the Sabbath – in the Ten Commandments, for example – as a day of rest appointed by God, to be kept holy, is also binding for the Christian Sunday. His conclusion is that "Sabbath and Sunday have nothing in common."[6] I know that Protestants by no means universally accept this opinion,[7] but the view does exist. It seems that theological controversy is bound to arise when the discussion turns to subjects of such existential importance as festivals. Karl Kerényi once remarked that the great Anglo-Saxon ethnologists of the turn of the century had completely overlooked the phenomenon of festivals, despite their conspicuous part in all primitive cultures. He rather surprisingly explained this curious blind spot as a consequence of the mentality of the "great *Protestant* cultures."[8] For my part, I do not propose to become involved in controversial theological problems, nor in theology at all. I mention these matters only in order to state my own premises as clearly as possible, for they too are inevitably theological in nature. My assumptions are: first, that the Old Testament Sabbath entered into the Christian Sunday and was "absorbed" by it; and second, that consequently Sunday, like the Sabbath, must be conceived as, to put it most cautiously, an institution not altogether established by men. Both days represent the Biblical Seventh Day, the *requies Domini Dei tui* (Deut. 5, 14), the divine day of rest on which not only master and servant but even the cattle are to rest. The Decalogue, incidentally, adds another note that nowadays strikes us in terms of the greatest immediacy – a reference to political servitude: "Remember that you were a servant in the land of Egypt, and the Lord your God brought you out thence" (Deut. 5, 15).

The Seventh Day commemorates not only the completion of the divine work, but also the divine assent to Creation. It was on the Seventh Day that the prodigious words were spoken that everything was "very good." We cannot conceive a more radical, a deeper-lying justification of the essential goodness of all reality than this, that God Himself, in bringing things into being, affirms and loves these very same things, all of them without exception. And to man also, insofar as he accepts it, this is the uttermost legitimation – perhaps I should also say, the ultimate encouragement which alone is unassailable, likewise to find the things of the world good, in spite of everything. And therefore it is also legitimation and encouragement to celebrate festivals festively.

During the great autumn festivals in Bengal I asked quite a few persons whether they could tell me the reason for their present festive joy. The answer of one orthodox Hindu ran: It is the joy of being a creature whom God has created out of joy.

But this is the very thing, the "gift of being

created," which is celebrated on Sunday, says Thomas Aquinas.[9] This *beneficium creationis*, he says, is the "first and foremost" of all divine gifts.[10] Thus he portrays Sunday as the model of all festive celebration. On that day we particularly celebrate what underlies all other times of festivity: assent to Creation.

At the same time, however, the Seventh Day has always been conceived as a symbol pointing ahead, a prefiguring of the "last and foremost" to divine gift, the eternal peace of God coming to all beings. Sunday is dedicated to this hope; the day itself becomes "an image of the coming age," "*imago venturi saeculi.*"[11]

Thus the holiday and day of worship for Christendom, recurring every week, is meant to serve both to recall the beginning of Creation and to herald future bliss. And in thus summoning before the soul's vision both the beginning and the end of time,[12] it throws open that wide, that infinite horizon which the great festivals must have for their full celebration.

Plainly, it is an extraordinary demand that such an interpretation of Sunday makes upon the average man. Some may call it an excessive demand, although it is scarcely more challenging than the task of meeting the demands of being human. At any rate, this precise interpretation, which does not draw any romantic veil over the measurements of reality, shows men one clearly drawn potentiality of their psychic life. And perhaps the average man, some time when he is thrown back upon his last resources, will be forced to recognize this potentiality as his own. And with that recognition will come, perhaps, a great sense of freedom and relief.

Nevertheless, this "Lord's day," *dies Dominica,* is not a specifically Christian holiday, insofar as it fulfills the Old Testament Sabbath, the Seventh Day. What makes Sunday Christian is its relation to Christ, its celebration of God's Incarnation, which reached its full fruit and revelation in the Resurrection of the Lord. The Christian Sunday is an emanation of Easter.

Easter itself, although it celebrates a historical event, could never be a real festival, let alone *"the* festival of the Church,"[13] if it were not something more than and different from a mere memorial day. What is in truth involved is a mysterious contemporizing of this event, which evokes an incomparably more real present than memory ever can (although it is also true that "a pleasure is full grown only when it is remembered"[14]). What is more, the reason and occasion for this festival is that in Christ's Resurrection something began by which man's life ever since, and today and for all the future, received that incomprehensible exaltation that the language of theology calls Grace and New Life. And therefore in the Christian celebration of Easter quite particularly an affirmation of the whole of existence is experienced and celebrated. No more rightful, more comprehensive and fundamental an affirmation can be conceived.

The gift of having been created, the promise of perfect bliss, the communication of divine vitality through Incarnation and Resurrection – all these are things, we might say, which determine human life every hour of every day, if the Christians are right. Why, then, are they "celebrated" only now and again, only every seventh day, or only on the rare great feast days? As we see, once again the theme of "everlasting festival" comes into view. In point of fact festivals could not be celebrated as special, rare, and exceptional days, and celebrated spontaneously, if the festive occasion did not exist continually and without cessation and were not so experienced (as the receiving of something be-loved). If any specific day is to be singled out from the rest and celebrated as a festival, this can only be done as the manifestation of a perpetual though hidden festivity.

This idea is not limited to the Christian realm, although in that realm we find it expressed with particular stress: "We spend our whole lives like a feast day";[15] "we have unending holiday";[16] "ours . . . is an eternal festival";[17] "*in domo Dei festivitas sempiterna est*"[18] – and so on. Pythagoras, too, called man's life a *panégyris*,[19] a festival. And in Plato's great late dialogue, *The Laws*, when the talk turns to the festivals to be celebrated in the ideal republic and the question is raised of how many there will be, the "Athenian" (Socrates) answers "There should be no less than three hundred and sixty-five of them,"[20] so that it will be possible to sacrifice to one of the gods every day (to which one modern German edition of Plato[21] makes the comment that this is a "pretty conceit"). The same basic conception is also to be found in ancient Rome; one of the highest priests, the *Flamen Dialis*, was spoken of as *cotidie feriatus*,[22] one who celebrated festivals every single day.

Even now, however little it may seem so on the surface, the latent presence of the everlasting festival constitutes one of the basic elements of these present times also.

VI

Within the same sentence in which Plato calls the recreation of festival divinely founded, he also says that the Muses were given to us as "festival companions."[1] And indeed, a festival without singing, music, dancing, without visible forms of celebration, without any kind of works of art, cannot be imagined. But what we find is a surprisingly many-stranded relationship linking the arts to festivity.

First of all, the artistic act is like festivity itself, something out of the ordinary, something unusual, which is not covered by the rules governing the workaday world. This is true not only of the artist's creative act, which gives rise to the work of art, but also of the secondary act of the person who (for example) reads a poem poetically. Both events depend upon "being struck by the lightning-flash of vision," and both "stand out of the flow of existence much as festivals stand out of the chain of almost indistinguishable days."[2] Both are rather rare; both have an "insular" character.[3]

It should be clear, moreover, that the invisible aspect of festivity, the praise of the world which lies at a festival's innermost core, can attain a physical form, can be made perceptible to the senses, only through the medium of the arts. Also, the effect of festivity, the stepping out of time and the refreshment that penetrates to the depths of the soul, reaches the celebrant in the form of a message couched in the language of the arts. "The emergence of festivity," says Friedrich Schleiermacher,[4] "can take place only through art."

Because this is so, the fine arts keep alive the memory of the true ritualistic, religious origins of festivals when these begin to wither or be forgotten. And this memory may at some moment succeed in blasting open again the buried entrance. Thus there is a goodly amount of truth in the rather excessive statement that only "through and by way of poetry" can we still know,[5] if at all, what a festival is.

On the other hand, the very overestimation of the arts can also obscure this knowledge. The fact that the arts have their natural place within festivals indicates that they are not themselves the festivals. Rather, the arts, like pleasure itself, are derivative and secondary; they are a contribution, the adornment and medium of the festival, but not its substance. As soon as festiveness itself becomes unachievable, the arts are inevitably left without a home; their inner necessity and even their credibility fade away. That is a state of affairs that great artists have naturally become conscious of, insofar as they have a concern for the fundamentals of their own métier, although perhaps they only see the problem but do not perceive its cause, and give voice only to their perplexity. Gottfried Benn,[6] for instance, has asked what all the effort toward perfection is ultimately all about "If something is finished, it must be perfect – true, but what then?" He does not answer the question; probably he knows no answer.

It is not too surprising that under conditions of tyranny the arts fall into the service of the political power and are subjected to utilitarian ends – quite often with the acquiescence of the artists themselves. What it amounts to is that homeless art looks for a new home. We can see why, shortly after the Second World War, a well-known German composer said that modern music could regain its health only as "utilitarian music." Musicians, perhaps, should accept commissions to write music for political demonstrations, he argued: after all, Johann Sebastian Bach had also "written almost exclusively utilitarian pieces."[7] The reference to Bach, of course, reveals the utterly hopeless error underlying this thesis – as if there were no difference between art's serving political and economic ends on the one hand, and its place within the festivals of public worship. Such service is not merely serving ends; on the contrary, it is the highest and perhaps the only way for art to be completely itself and to arrive "autonomously" at its most essential goal: the praise of Creation. For in that, above all, the arts and festivity join hands; both are nourished by affirmation of Creation.

Let us stress again that this affirmation is not the same thing as approval of any pragmatic situation. Often enough, pragmatic states are characterized by their *lack* of reality. Rather, what is meant is affirmation of the true creaturely Being of the world, of things and of man, the Being on which all pragmatic states rest. There can be neither festivals nor fine arts without that prior affirmation, the nature of which is perhaps best conveyed by that great word: love. Normally, the word should be used sparingly, but in this case it is the exact term we want. *"C'est l'amour qui chante"*;[8] only the lover sings; without love we cannot expect song. "Song" here stands not only for poetry and, of course, music, but also for the utterances and works of all the fine arts taken together. Elegy, too, is song.[9] And insofar as tragedy, *poésie noire* and *peinture noire*, as well as even the most unsparing satire, rightfully deserve the proud name of true works of art, they necessarily draw their vitality from consent to the true reality. For what else is mourned as disaster and misfortune, what is denounced as shameful, what is execrated, questioned, ridiculed, or else pictured as a terrible, threatening possibility – what, if not the decay, the destruction, and the effacement of that same true reality? Evidently, that true reality is really accepted and affirmed as the standard and the court of last appeal. The great work of art, at any rate, always remains within all these negations "the affirmation of affirmations that comprehends all assents within itself."[10] And therein lies its kinship with festivity.

Even language itself, to the extent that it conceals song within itself, as the Romans put it (*"est etiam in dicendo quidam cantus obscurior"*[11]) – or to express this differently, to the extent that it is not mere communication for practical ends, but simple naming, "useless" and independent denomination of what is – even that distinctively human achievement which is called language seems to spring into being within the same free realm that is created by the festival. "The festal origin of human speech" – a surprising concept! All the same, it has been defended with rather considerable arguments.[12] Here again we detect a strand in the reciprocal relation of festivity and the fine arts, which may be seen as merely different "dialects" of man's obscurely "singing" speech.

Wherever assent to the world is expressly rejected, expressly and consistently (though this last is not easy), the root of both festivity and the arts is destroyed. Gloomy diagnosticians told us long ago that in an existence founded on negation, festivity becomes a caricature of itself. Nietzsche says that all festivals are nothing but "spectacles without spectators, tables full of gifts without recipients."[13] Schopenhauer speaks of "mere appearance"; "the essence of the thing is lacking"; joy is "usually not to be found; it alone has canceled its appearance at the festival."[14] And Kurt Eisner's brilliant and confused pamphlet of 1906, *Feste der Festlosen* ("Festivals of the Unfestive"), whose title sums up the whole argument, contains this sentence: "Perhaps the time is approaching when festivals as mass manifestations of an intensified sense of life will be nothing more than curiosities to be studied from old pictures and artifacts preserved in ethnological museums."[15] Such remarks are not without foundation, even though a number of "positive" arguments against them can be cited. At any rate, their symptomatic value is incontestable.

As for the situation of the arts, that too is a complex matter not easily penetrated, let alone judged. It is indubitably true that refusal of assent makes "song" impossible. If assent to the world can no longer be celebrated festively at all, then every one of the fine arts becomes homeless, useless, idle, unbelievable, and at bottom impossible. To be sure, such refusal can exist side by side with the greatest technical skill. That is precisely what complicates the matter. For wherever truthful form is achieved, no matter how "formalistic" it may be, there exists *eo ipso* in some sense harmony, concord with a pre-established image of order – and thus inevitably a grain of affirmation. Complete negation is necessarily formless; it presupposes the shattering of form; whereas negation proclaimed in perfect form is only a half-negation, inherently a contradiction of itself. And in fact, the arts of our time are characterized by such abstrusities of structure, quite aside from the fact that a good deal of art that pretends to metaphysical negation is really founded upon assent to a hidden order. Nevertheless, it is just as clear that there runs through all varieties of art a resolute refusal to accept the "absurd" world. So keen a student of literature as Ernst Robert Curtius has said that the literature of the past hundred years has chiefly been a form of "cultivated censure," a category that includes all "that twenty or thirty naturalisms, expressionisms, existentialisms in all countries and continents have accumulated as incriminating evidence against man, life, being in general."[16] And no one is likely to deny that the hopelessness, as well as the simple absence of reality so widespread in the realm of the arts, is rooted in this incapacity to affirm, or the deliberate refusal to do so, no matter in what specific terms the negation is couched.

Worse than clear negation, however, is mendacious affirmation. Worse than the silencing and stifling of festivity and the arts is sham practicing of them. And once again we may see that pseudo-art is related in a variety of ways to pseudo-festivity. The sham is inherent in the fact that the affirmation and assent compatible only with true reality is falsified into a smug yea-saying, whose basic element is a desire to fend off reality, so as not to be disturbed, at any price. A deceptive escape from the narrowness of the workaday utilitarian world is found in the form of entertainment and "forgetting ones worries." And the same mendacious message also reaches men through the medium of the pseudo-arts, whether trivial or pretentious, flattering or entertaining, or intoxicating like a drug. Man craves by nature to enter the "other" world, but he can attain it only if true festivity truly comes to pass. For it appears – but it is appearance only – that this other dimension of reality can be produced with ease and at will; it *appears* to stand at the disposal of the harried or bored man who needs "entertainment" and a "change." And the Sophist, the producer of fictive reality,[17] has his day.

But the man who by such devices is the more imprisoned within a workaday world now made amusing no longer misses real festivity; he does not notice the emptiness. And thus he even stops grieving over his loss – and the loss thereby is finally sealed.

This is the process by which an age is changed into a "period of dearth." Hölderlin's great poem, *Bread and Wine*, from which we take the phrase, points the moral in verses of almost painful beauty.[18] Though there may be some minor variations in the interpretation of detail, the meaning of the poem as a whole is quite clear: the true existential poverty of man consists in his having lost the power to celebrate a festival festively. And Hölderlin leaves no room for doubt that he is speaking of the festivals of ritual worship, whose "crowns" are the gods.

But as for the question, "And what are poets for in a period of dearth?" – it is, of course, a question that carries its own answer within itself, much as if someone were to say: What are festival companions for if there is no festival?

VII

Lao-tzu[1] has said that a man is not sick so long as
sickness sickens him. Hence, things have not
reached their sorriest pass as long as men are concerned over the disappearance of the festive principle from life. By the same token, the grumblings
of cultural critics and the plaints of poets are the
very opposite of hopelessness. But when, unno-
ticed and almost unnoticeable, sham festivals foist
themselves on men in place of true festivity (as Socrates describes the flattering falsehood of the
Sophists: It uses pleasure as a bait to catch folly
and pretends to be that which it simulates[2]) – then
the situation is really bad. Apparently there have
been sham festivals all through the ages; decadence of festivity is an ever-present danger. The
Late Roman Empire, for example, was rife with
festal arrangements lacking the truly festive core,
"les attributs de la fête sans le jour de la fête"[3] – a typical phenomenon of a declining society. Naturally
enough, in the past as well as in the present, the
festivals most prone to such corruption have been
those whose public character is unassailable. Even
secularized society cannot – not yet – ignore
Christmas. However, as everyone has observed,

the real festival is almost disappearing behind the commercialized folderol that has come to the fore. The true content sometimes becomes distorted to a degree that is really grotesque. In Japan the opinion has been voiced in all seriousness that commercial advertising is not misusing the symbols of the Christmas festival, but rather that the Christian holiday has borrowed the various motifs so successful in the department store displays, in order to exert a more powerful influence on the public.[4] In spite of all such nonsense, of course, both in Japan and elsewhere, the real Christmas continues to be celebrated undisturbed as the festival of God's Incarnation, Perhaps, however, the celebration is tending more and more to be non-public (although on the other hand this festival, like ritual worship in general, demands publicness, is "in itself" a public act). Which again shows how hard it is to arrive at dogmatic judgments about what festivals really are in human society.

Compared with the falsification, by the multiplying of pseudo-festive trappings, of festivals already existing as institutions, the creation of completely new festivals on the basis of a legislative act, *feria ex senatus consulto*, is a relatively unambiguous problem, although those closely involved may find it difficult to see through the illusion. Granted, all festivals in one sense are "made" by men – not only celebrated but also instituted. Almost everything about festivals, including the great and traditional ones, is indubitably the result of human arrangements, from the fixing of a particular calendar day[5] to the specific forms of the sacrifices, the ceremonies, the parades, and so on. Human institutions, then. Nevertheless, the Biblical sentence remains inviolate: that the festival is a day "the Lord has made" (Ps. 117, 24). It remains true because while man can make the celebration, he cannot make what is to be celebrated, cannot make the festive occasion and the cause for celebrating. The happiness of being created, the existential goodness of things, the participation in the life of God, the overcoming of death – all these occasions of the great traditional festivals are pure gift. But because no one can confer a gift on himself, something that is entirely a human institution cannot be a real festival.

On the other hand, wherever in the course of history we encounter artificial holidays, we may conclude that they point to a particular interpretation of man's being: to the claim that man, especially in the exercise of political power, is able to bring about his own salvation as well as that of the world. Proof of such lofty powers can always be simulated, provided political propaganda tries hard enough. The semblance can even be kept up, at any rate for a while. And on the basis of it artificial festivals, likewise for a time at least, can thrive and even exert a more or less convincing spell – especially if the combined powers of the pseudo-arts, entertainment, sensationalism, and manipulated illusion are brought to bear, and if in addition the political rulers command and control such "spontaneous festive gladness."

We also have what we may call milder prototypes of the artificial holiday which do not contrast so strongly with the traditional festivals. Such, for example, are the whole assortment of political memorial days, insofar as they are conceived as festivals – ranging from the Athenian memorials for the victories of Marathon and Salamis to the anniversary of the Battle of Sedan in Wilhelmine Germany[6] and the Nazi November 9 rallies celebrating Hitler's 1923 Munich "putsch." The category also includes the courtly festivals of the Renaissance and Baroque periods, which, incidentally, were for the most part imitations of classical festivals. The costly[7] but empty pomp of their processions, fireworks, equestrian ballets, and orchestras concealed in pastries[8] were admittedly designed[9] chiefly to testify to the magnificence of their sponsors. Such display is rather neutral, since it is merely harmless playfulness (although it is of dubious value for that reason). Moreover, these events were never meant to compete with the traditional festivals of ritual worship – although the latter, of course, could not help being affected by them.

This habit of inventing festivals took a serious turn only when, in the course of the French Revolution, entirely new festivals were initiated by the state. These were intended to displace and replace the traditional religious holidays, although that tendency only gradually gathered strength during the Revolution. In 1791 Mass was still celebrated at the July 14 festival, with "altars of the fatherland" erected everywhere.[10] In Paris, incidentally, the celebrant was the newly appointed Bishop Jean Baptiste Gobel, whose life had the elements of tragedy.[11] (In 1789, an ambitious suffragan bishop and member of the National Assembly, he approved all the anti-religious measures of the Revolution. Later, under pressure, he "voluntarily" renounced all his offices "as servant of the Catholic cult," and six months later, in April 1794, under Robespierre, who officially introduced the cult of the Supreme Being, he was charged with atheism and executed. He died crying: "Long live Christ.") The very next year, 1792, priests were no longer allowed to take part in such celebrations, not even the priests who had "fallen in line." Shortly before the famous Festival of Reason in the Cathedral of Notre Dame (November 10, 1793) the Commune of Paris banned all acts of public worship of the traditional kind.[12] When the Parisian artists celebrated the planting of one of the countless Trees of Liberty, they sang a parody, composed by François Joseph Gossec, of the hymn "O Salutaris Hostia."[13]

A characteristic trait of the new festivals was their coercive nature. Those who did not participate made themselves suspect. It is still so today. Several days beforehand, the citizen may read in the newspaper[14] what is expected of him: "When the bells ring, all will leave their houses, which will be entrusted to the protection of the law and

Republican virtues. The populace will fill the streets and public squares, aflame with joy and fraternity ..." and so on. Naturally, that sort of thing is not a gentle appeal for the friendly co-operation of the public; it is an edict. And thenceforth the element of political coercion and propagandistic intimidation remained an essential part of the artificial festival. Acts which would be meaningful only as spontaneous gestures were organized and ordered; they became institutions intended to demonstrate political reliability. This led inevitably to a pervasive, constitutional dishonesty which ever since has been another of the characteristic signs of the artificial holiday. There is no way to tell whether participation in them is a measure of self-protection, because not to participate would be politically dangerous, or whether it is a conditioned response to the deafening blare or a propaganda machine that has taken over every agency of communication. Even the participant himself can scarcely say how he "really" feels about it – this may sound incredible, but not to those who know ideologically based despotisms from the inside.

Contemporary accounts of the festivals of the French Revolution reek of boredom, the infinite boredom of utter unreality, which makes the reading of them a startling experience. The "extravagant expenditure ... on pinchbeck symbolical properties, on plaster, cardboard, and tin,"[15] the bombastic declamation of platitudes, the empty histrionics of the pseudo-liturgy emanate a ghostly unreality. At the translation of the body of "Saint Voltaire,"[16] "the first philosophical festival"[17] of the Revolution, young men in the costume of ancient Romans accompanied the sarcophagus to the Pantheon. From the altar of the fatherland the Mayor of Paris displayed the book containing the Constitution, holding it out to his fellow citizens like a monstrance. A girl ignited a Bengal light, by means of a magnifying glass producing the "holy fire," which then flared up from a Greek vase in the hues of the Tricolor.[18] The painter Jacques Louis David, the canny stage manager of almost all the great Festivals of the Revolution (and incidentally the representative of a numerous band of painters, sculptors, poets, and musicians who clamored to be "appointed" – and paid – by the new rulers[19]), went to the Convention in the summer of 1793 with a plan for a festival of the "fraternity of all Frenchmen." It was instantly accepted and the show swiftly put on. Among its features were the following: A procession marched to the site of the Bastille, where the President of the Convention was the first to drink water jetting from the breasts of a monumental female figure ("Nature as the Fountain of Rebirth"), after first sprinkling the statue of the "Sun of Freedom" erected beside her. Incidentally, he drank from an agate cup which, as the Convention Minutes stipulated, was to be placed in the National Museum with an inscription to remind posterity of its "exalted use."[20] At the moment of this solemn act three thousand caged birds were released, tagged with ribbons hearing the inscription: "We are free – imitate us!"[21]

New proposals for such celebrations were constantly being placed before the National Assembly.[22] The details of these are significant though they tend to be slurred over in most accounts. Therefore I take the liberty of sketching two such affairs, one belonging to the category of "victory celebration," while the other was intended as a specifically religious festival.

In June 1790, after the first anniversary of the Revolution was celebrated with a mass meeting in Versailles, the participants marched back to Paris in a gigantic parade. A banquet was held en route in the Bois de Boulogne, and served by young "patriotic nymphs." Here the President read aloud, as a kind of grace, the first two articles of the Rights of Man, to which the banqueters responded: "Amen." There were toasts not only to freedom but also to the happiness of the whole universe, "*au bonheur de l'univers entier.*" Women dressed as shepherdesses crowned the Deputies of the National Assembly, including Robespierre, with wreaths of oak leaves. Finally a replica of the Bastille – presumably made of papier-mâché – was carried in and set down. Soldiers of the National Guard promptly drew their swords and hacked the abhorred structure to pieces. But behold, from the ruins a white-clad child emerged, as well as several copies of the Declaration of the Rights of Man and selected volumes of Rousseau's works.[23]

Robespierre's famous "anti-atheistic" speech of May 7, 1794, proclaimed thirty-six new days of national festival which, as he said, were to be "the mightiest means of rebirth." The most important was the "Festival of the Supreme Being," celebrated for the first time on June 8, 1794, again staged by Jacques Louis David. The proper forms of festive rejoicing were published the day before in the newspapers: "Friends, brothers, spouses, old people are to embrace one another. Mothers will carry bouquets of roses in their hands. Fathers will lead their sword-bearing sons, each holding an oak branch." There was to be a festive procession, with speeches and solemn ceremonies at various halting places. The "liturgist" of these ceremonies was Robespierre in person. Thus, at the conclusion of a speech at the Tuileries, he ordered a mighty statue of Atheism constructed of inflammable material to be set afire. The flames were to reveal an equally enormous statue of Wisdom. (Because of a technical slip the latter appeared badly smoke-blackened – which was regarded by many as an evil omen.[24]) At the concluding celebration on the Champ de Mars a hymn was sung, the last stanza in chorus. "Simultaneously" – I am quoting the account of the *Moniteur* – "the girls tossed flowers on high; the young men drew their swords and swore to make their weapons victorious everywhere. The old men placed their hands on the young men's heads and gave them their paternal blessing. Finally a detachment of artillery, 'arm of national vengeance,' fired into the air, and all citizens and citizenesses, expressing their feelings in fraternal embraces, ended the festival by the resounding cry of humanity and civic conscience: 'Long live the Republic!'"[25]

"A tragic operetta," all this has been called.[26] But such epithets do not do justice to the true evil and hopelessness of this lustily celebrated nonsense.

For the place in life which should naturally be occupied by real festivity cannot remain empty. And when real festivals are no longer celebrated, for whatever reasons, the susceptibility to artificial festivals grows. With the exception of the one essential that alone makes a festival truly festive, all other outward attributes of festivity may indeed be found in the imitation brand. Oddly enough, in fact, some of the basic features of festivals in general, which otherwise tend too often to be neglected, are stressed in sham festivals. For instance: ideally speaking, festivals should be public affairs of concern to the political community; during festivals social differences should he abolished;[27] social and political peace, real "fraternization," should be considered the fruits, or even the preconditions, of festivals. From time immemorial men have felt that this last element is essential to festivity. Pindar[28] speaks of "Zeus's messengers of peace" who went about throughout Greece as the Olympic Games approached, calling for the truce without which there could be no celebration; and when, under Constantine, the politically liberated Christians set about establishing the official form of the Sunday holiday, almost the first stipulation was that on that day no violence must be done, not even to criminals.[29] It is startling that an element which belongs so properly to real festivals should be adopted by the makers of artificial holidays and become part of their agenda. To be sure, in practice the principle is spoiled by lies and violence.

The fundamental vapidness of these artificial festivals is clearly exposed when we try to find out *what* they are actually celebrating. What is the object, the reason, the occasion? A phrase that recurs so constantly in the literature of revolution[30] as to be virtually a classic formula maintains that the people themselves are not only the "ornament" of the festival and its organizers, but also its object. As might be imagined, this phrase, too, goes back to Rousseau. The object of the festivals celebrated by "happy peoples," he says, is, "if you will, nothing at all"; strictly speaking, however, the people themselves are the festive spectacle.[31] But these remarks are still too imprecise; the decisive factor is still unsaid: that what is really being celebrated is human "happiness," either already achieved or to be achieved by change in social conditions at the instance of the political power. The Legislative Assembly looked upon itself, according to an official document of 1792, as a union of "philosophers" occupied with preparing the "happiness of the world."[32] The ideologists of the Revolution considered the legislator a "priest of social felicity,"[33] engaged upon an unending program of reshaping and improving the social conditions of human life.

At this point in our discussion we may expect a double objection. First, someone may say: Really now, what is wrong with trying to ameliorate the conditions of human life by, among other things, modifying the social organization? To this, we can answer very briefly: There is nothing wrong with it. The second argument, which strikes more closely at the point in question, might be put as follows: Is not the enthusiastic hailing of life and the world, so evident in all these Revolutionary festivals, exactly what has been proclaimed as the necessary prerequisite for festivity? Did not these revolutionaries have an exceedingly optimistic view of man? Why, then, is it impossible for a real festival to be celebrated on that basis? What is lacking?

This question calls for an explicit answer. Here it is; There can be no festivity when man, imagining himself self-sufficient, refuses to recognize that Goodness of things which goes far beyond any conceivable utility; it is the Goodness of reality taken as a whole which validates all other particular goods and which man himself can never produce nor simply translate into social or individual "welfare." He truly receives it only when he accepts it as pure gift. The only fitting way to respond to such gift is by praise of God in ritual worship. In short, it is the withholding of public worship that makes festivity wither at the root.

And yet we cannot say that the French Revolution as a historical event ushered in the obverse of true festivity. True, we can see the beginnings of that obverse in the Revolution's festivals, but it did not reach its apogee. The unrealistic extravagance of these fêtes, their bombast and enthusiasm, are evidence that the society that launched them had not arrived at the purest form of rationally calculated utility. Only when that point is reached can we say that festivity itself, not just a particular variety of festivity, has been negated in principle. This negation was reserved for a later, more consistent age in which the "transformation of the individual into the worker"[34] would be completed and the romantic notion of "priests of social felicity" would be supplanted by the more brutal standard of the social engineer.

VIII

When the American Federation of Labor decided
to set May 1, 1886, as the target date for winning
the eight-hour day, which it had been demanding
for years, the only thing in favor of the first of May
was that it was moving day, the usual date when
leases and other economic agreements ran out.
There was no talk of mythical "spring festivals"[1]
or other ideas rooted in folklore. The employers
opposed the demand, and so a strike was called for
that day. At a demonstration in Chicago a bomb
was thrown – by whom was never known. The po-
lice fired into the crowd, killing and wounding
several of the demonstrators. The labor leaders
charged with instigating the demonstration were
tried in an atmosphere of hatred and hysteria;
seven were sentenced to death and four executed.
In memory of these martyrs of the labor move-
ment, the first of May was adopted internationally
as a day given over to demonstrating for shorter
working hours.[2] Only five years later did the International Labor Congress in Brussels declare it a
"festival day" for the first time. In so doing, the
Congress started something quite new, with un-
foreseeable consequences, which ultimately caused

the original historical occasion to be completely forgotten. But the latent spirit of the original decision comes to the fore in the May Day celebrations of totalitarian governments. The wording of the Brussels resolution of 1891 was as, follows: "In order to preserve to the first of May its specific economic character, that of the demand for the eight-hour day and of proclamation of the class struggle, the Congress resolves: The first of May is a festival day shared by the workers of all countries, on which the workers shall demonstrate their solidarity and their shared demands. This festival day should be pronounced a day of rest... ."[3]

It seems to me that two things in this program deserve particular attention: first, that an economic occasion in the class struggle is declared a "festival day" as if that were a matter of course; and second, the fact that the new element of "strike" is boldly tacked on to the old idea of a "day of rest." May first is "a rehearsal for the general strike," Aristide Briand said.[4] To be sure, a good many "resolutions" continued to speak in traditional language of a "day of rest" as "the worthiest form of celebration."[5] However, such a leader as Viktor Adler[6] declared bluntly that only by stopping work could "the agitational character of May first as a truly proletarian and revolutionary demonstration" be preserved – for which reason the more radical Syndicalists of the Latin countries rejected the term "holiday" as romantic.[7]

At the same time the posters and banners

carried in the processions[8] ("This is the day the *people* made; it is hallowed throughout the world"; "Socialism, thy kingdom come!"; "Our Pentecost, when the power of the Holy Spirit of Socialism rushes through the world, making converts"), and the propaganda pamphlets and leaflets distributed in honor of the "festival," proclaim the "stalwart will of the working class no longer to let bourgeois society alone determine what shall be the workdays and what shall be the feast."[9] Thus the traditional festivals are rejected as bourgeois institutions. Kurt Eisner said of the May first "festival of the peoples" that "the mighty rhythm of its idea proclaims a golden age of work and rejoicing as a goal to be immediately achieved; and it is this which raises it far above all secular and religious, pagan and Christian festivals of the past."[10]

Once again it must be said that all these examples are more or less innocent preludes of what is to come. The thing becomes serious when the Bolshevist regime takes over the "socialist holiday." For the day can then no longer retain the character of a demonstration against the existing order. The existing order has become identical with the dictatorship of the proletariat. What, then, is to be done with the first of May? It is turned into something quite unexpected, though surprising only to those who do not have an adequate conception of the nature of the totalitarian labor state. The first of May becomes, to put it briefly, a day that differs from all other workdays and rest days of the year in that it is celebrated

by – additional, voluntary, unpaid work! In lieu of
the demand for a *shorter* workday, which in the past
had been the justification and the meaning of the
day, the workers are asked to accept the very opposite, "the idea of *prolongation* of work." From that, as
an official pronouncement[11] put it, there develops
gradually "the voluntary work of the progressive
elements of the working class, the Communists."
The "rehearsal for the general strike" is forgotten.
"This holiday is one of general work" (thus Leon
Trotsky).[12] And Maxim Gorky: "It is a wonderful
idea to make the spring festival of the workers a
holiday of voluntary work."[13]

The sentences I have quoted come from a joint
proclamation, issued in 1920 and signed by Lenin,
Kalinin, Bukharin, and almost all the great names
of Bolshevism, in an attempt to put across this
new meaning of the May first celebration.

Naturally, the "voluntary" nature of this holiday work must be understood in a propaganda
sense. And no one versed in the instrumentation of
such "revolutionary" rhetoric would fail to hear the
overtones of threat. It was Lenin himself who said:
"Only people who have sold themselves to capital-
ism are capable of condemning the use of the great
May holiday for our mass effort to introduce Com-
munist work."[14] Gorky ruled that it was a "crime
not to understand" the purpose of giving that particular form to the holiday.[15] The phrase "labor de-
serter" begins to be bandied about, and we are told
that "the most progressive ranks of the proletariat

will use force in order finally to eliminate . . . the passive resistance" of such deserters. The time for such a reckoning would come when "we have advanced organizationally to the point that the entire population is comprehended ... in one single labor army."[16] After such hints, the authorities could be fairly sure that their suggestion would be eagerly taken up. When the officials and scientists of the Moscow government ministries marched out to till the fields "belonging to the Commune," the peasants of the vicinity flocked to the place "to see how the proletariat celebrates its labor holiday."[17]

We must call to mind again that this language of intimidation is being used to proclaim a *festival* – or rather, to proclaim an institution which according to the "language rules" of a dictatorship continues to be called a "holiday," in mockery of every meaning of the word.

Incidentally, that heroic effort of 1920 was not sustained. Instead, still another meaning soon came to the fore. From 1922[18] on, May first became more and more exclusively a day on which the Soviet Union displayed its military strength in gigantic parades. The already quoted remark[19] in regard to the Baroque court festivals is apt enough, in this case the May Day celebration serves chiefly to demonstrate the *grandeur* of its sponsors.

The very same was true of the gigantic May Day celebrations of the Nazi regime. The sumptuousness of the arrangements for the vast demonstrations staged between 1933 and 1936 in Berlin's Tempelhof

Field (the "greatest demonstration ever seen in the history of the world"[20]) undoubtedly put into the shade both the Baroque festivals and Jacques Louis David's impresario achievements. But the coercive character of those demonstrations was likewise scarcely hidden. There were not many persons in Germany who could afford to stay away from the parties and parades. And we will not be surprised to find injunctions being issued that strongly recall the festivals of the French Revolution. Several days prior to May first, the state propaganda machine would publish the following instructions: "Decorate your houses and the streets of the cities and villages with fresh greenery and with the colors of the Reich! ... No train and no streetcar is to ride through Germany that is not decorated with flowers and greenery! The public buildings, railroad stations, post offices, and telegraph offices are to burgeon out in fresh greenery!"[21] So faithfully were these suggestions followed that German cities, large or small, could scarcely be distinguished, on that day, from Italian or Spanish cities decorated for Corpus Christi Day or for the festival of a patron saint. The emptiness of the rhetoric that spouted constantly from the loudspeakers, however, often descended to sheer gibberish: "My will – this we must all profess – is your faith!"[22]

The only reality hidden behind the bombast and empty spectacle was, just as in the Soviet state, the total subjection of human beings to work. It was, in fact, on the "holiday of labor" in

1935 that the "Labor Service" was announced, amid tumultuous applause from the "celebrants" – among them those affected by the decree. And then the same shift in meaning took place once again: in National Socialist Germany, May first, which incidentally was renamed as early as 1934 "National Holiday of the German People," became the prime occasion for striking displays of weapons of destruction, which the regime was already accumulating in preparation for total war.

The grim conclusion we may come to from all this is: The artificial holiday is not only a sham festival; it borders so dangerously on counterfestivity that it can abruptly be reversed into "antifestival."

IX

"C'est la guerre, qui correspond à la fête": the modern equivalent of festivals is war. In this provocative sentence Roger Caillois[1] answers the question of what nowadays takes that place in the life of society which once upon a time was filled by festivals. At first, he says, he imagined that the answer might be "vacations." But then he realized that vacations are not only not consonant with festivals, but that they are, rather, mutually exclusive; and that in the present world it is, instead, war that fulfills the functions of the great festivals. In war, he says, all the attributes of festivals may be found (he considers festivals as essentially "a time of excess"): the most drastic conversion and consumption of energies, the eruption of stored force, the merging of the individual in the totality, the squandering of resources ordinarily carefully husbanded, the wild breaking down of inhibitions – and so on.

Once we have recovered from the shock that such a statement is meant to inflict upon the reader, once we begin casting about for counterarguments, we are forced to admit, however much against our will, that the present state of things does seem to favor so extreme a hypothesis. Since the time of Nietzsche, who called himself "the destroyer par excellence"[2] and who dreamed of a company of men who would be called "destroyers"[3] – for almost three generations, then, the idea of "active nihilism,"[4] of the "will to nothingness"[5] and "pleasure even in destruction,"[6] has been part of the modern attitude toward life. And when someone comments that a myth like that of the Twilight of the Gods, which implies the shattering of the created world, in our time no longer belongs solely to the realm of imagination,[7] we can scarcely disagree. Even Pierre Teilhard de Chardin, although enthusiastically convinced of the future energy of the Cosmos, feels called upon to speak of a dawning "organic crisis in evolution" which is preparing "under our modern disquiet." The last century, he says,[8] witnessed the first systematic strikes in industry; "the next will surely not pass without the threat of strikes in the noosphere." "Or more precisely, there is a danger that the world should refuse itself when perceiving itself through reflection."

This "strike" has evidently already begun. "Darkening of the world," "flight of the gods,"[9] "disintegration of reality," "absurdity of existence," "nausea" – such are the key words heard on every hand, whether in philosophical or literary discussions, whether the subject be the visual arts or music. In the face of this overpowering chorus of naysayers, there seems little point in arguing the matter. They insist that they have been betrayed, and are consequently "wiser than the unbetrayed," in Kierkegaard's phrase.[10] "He who laughs has not yet received the terrible tidings."[11]

Not that the actual state of the world does not offer sufficient grounds for such fatalism. We might remember, for example, that the great teachers of Christendom were also far from being "conformists" who accepted the world as it was. On the contrary, they held that man has so shamefully disgraced the earth and himself and plunged both into such a deplorable state that return to nothingness, total *annihilatio*, might well appear an act of justice.[12] Compared with such a view, it is the height of naive optimism to believe that the evil in the world is a matter of specific social systems or "dark ages." To be sure, those same teachers also knew that no one is really able to revoke the act of Creation except the Creator Himself; and that He had created all things "so that they might be" (Wisd. 1,14).[13] I really do not know how an incorruptible mind, faced with the evil in the world, could keep from utter despair were it not for the logically tenable conviction that there is a divinely guaranteed Goodness of being which no amount of mischief can undermine. But that *is* the point of view of the man who sees the world as *creatura* – not to speak of the believer who is confident of a salvation that infinitely surpasses all creature goodness. Perhaps it is only thanks to such super-empirical certainties that man is able to assume the intellectually and existentially extremely demanding task of facing naked reality without resorting to the evasions either of euphemism or of slander. But of course, what counts is not primarily a matter of intellectual categories, nor the psychological capacity to endure tensions. What counts is truth. And might it not he the truth that the man who despairs, he in particular, has "not yet received" certain "tidings"?

This is not the place to discuss the arguments of nihilism. Our subject is festivity. But it is self-evident that those negations, as soon as they reach a certain degree of intensity, render true festivity impossible. At the same time – and this seems considerably less self-evident – they pave the way for something else: that the destruction of the world, for example in a global war of annihilation, is not feared as an unspeakable calamity, but anticipated as something to be desired, even "celebrated" as ordinarily only affirmations can be. Thus destruction becomes "antifestival," one of those "great uprisings" which Eisner has described as borrowing "the means from war and the mood from festivals."[14]

To shut our eyes to this development would mean repressing a whole dimension of reality. Such antifestive "affirmation of negation" has to be taken into account. This, too, lies within the nature of man as a historical creature.

Nevertheless, I repudiate the hypothesis of war as the modern equivalent of festivals. It is not merely an unpardonable simplification; it is downright wrong. Its greatest error lies in its implying that our present era is devoid of true festivals, and moreover must be so. In reality festivals are not only possible, but are still being celebrated.

However, a sociological and psychological analysis of Western society based on attitudes toward festivity would still bring to light a good many dubious phenomena. Above all this one that we would be hard put to find anywhere today the kind of great festival that, springing from the praise of God in ritual worship, includes everybody, permeates all spheres, and puts its stamp on all of public life. On the other hand, the general susceptibility to artificial holidays established by men has risen considerably, even if, as in the case of, say, Mother's Day, there is no background of political coercion. No less dangerous is the susceptibility to quickly available, virtually purchasable surrogates which convey a counterfeit of the things that can be had only in true festivals: rapture, oblivion of ills, a sense of harmony with the world. Furthermore, most of the traditional holidays of Christendom have become awkward occasions, and a few of the great Christian festivals have been taken over so completely by commercialism that their degeneracy is almost total. In addition, there is the multitude of festivities and parties based on the illusion that no particular occasion is needed for celebrating, just leisure time and a well-lined pocketbook. All this combines in preparing the soil for the noisy pomp of pseudo-festivals to be celebrated at the command of any despotism.

But this is not the whole picture. In this same contemporary world of ours there remains the indestructible (for otherwise human nature itself would have to be destroyed) gift innate in all men which impels them now and again to escape from the restricted sphere where they labor for their necessities and provide for their security – to escape not by mere forgetting, but by undeceived recollection of the greater, more real reality. Now, as always, the workaday world can be transcended in poetry and the other arts. In the shattering emotion of love, beyond the delusions of sensuality, men continue to find entrance to the still point of the turning world. Now, as always, the experience of death as man's destiny, if accepted with an open and unarmored heart, acquaints us with a dimension of existence which fosters a detachment from the immediate aims of practical life. Now, as always, the philosophical mind will react with awe to the mystery of being revealed in a grain of matter or a human face.

Of course, all such responses are not in themselves festivity. They are the postludes of festivity, but in the proper circumstances they could again become the preludes. All such modes of ascending out of the world of mere utility once arose from the soil of a festival perhaps long since faded or forgotten; and so they may, by virtue of their evocative power, once again become a step toward a new festival to be celebrated in the future. Consequently, for the sake of what prospects there are for true festivity in our time, it is essential to resist the sophistical corruption of the arts, the cheapening of eroticism, the degradation of death, as well as the tendency to make philosophy a textbook subject or an irresponsible juggling of big words.

The core and source of festivity itself remains inviolably present in the midst of society. This is as true today as it was a thousand years ago. It remains in the form of the praise given in ritual worship, which is literally performed at every hour of the day. By its nature that praise is a public act, a festival celebrated before the face of Creation,[15] whether its site is a catacomb or a prisoner's cell. And because the festive occasion pure and simple, the divine guarantee of the world and of human salvation, exists and remains true continuously, we may say that in essence one single everlasting festival is being celebrated – so that the distinction between holiday and workday appears to be quite erased.

But both the all-embracing publicness of the religious festival and the continuous presence of that festival remain veiled from empirical observation. In happier ages, the hidden element manifested itself in visible form in the great feast days on which the passage of workaday, utilitarian time came to a halt for a moment. In less fortunate periods, in which even rare holidays come to nothing for a great variety of reasons, festivity recedes to deeper concealment.

But what is hidden is nonetheless real. And those who are certain that the ever-bountiful source of all festive celebration remains unalterably present in the world, even though veiled, will regard the empirically patent unfestivity of this same world as not altogether hopeless. However, they will see it as a condition that is difficult to decipher and, above all, that is in suspense. Two extreme historical potentialities have equal chances: the latent everlasting festival may be made manifest, or the "antifestival" may develop in its most radical form.

The Christian, however, is convinced that no destructive action, no matter how thoroughgoing, even if it is fervently celebrated as a gruesome "antifestival," can ever corrode the substance of Creation. "Miraculously founded and more miraculously restored," it cannot be corrupted by the "will to nothingness." Thus there always remains the "festive occasion" which alone justifies and inspires celebration. It remains in force, forever undiminished. And not even the complete "success" of self-annihilation on the part of the human race, not even the complete "destruction of the earth,"[16] could stamp out true festival. To be sure, in that case it would be celebrated "not in this eon nor on earth." But basically this is true, as we have seen, even for the festivals we celebrate here and now, in this present historical time.

Such thoughts lead, of course, far beyond a philosophical study of festivity. And we have reached a boundary at which the philosophical mind must necessarily fall silent. But it would be no very exceptional case if this silence made it possible to hear – to hear a more than philosophical message.

NOTES

I

1   Cf. the remarks on pages 23, 37, and 64 on the "everlasting festival."

2   Richard Alewyn and Karl Sälzle, *Das grosse Welttheater: Die Epoche der höfischen Feste in Dokument und Deutung.* *Rowohlts Deutsche Enzyklopädie* (Hamburg, 1959), p. 13.

3   Albert Camus, *The Myth of Sisyphus and Other Essays.* Translated from the French by Justin O'Brien (New York, Alfred A. Knopf, 1955), p. 123.

4   Bernard of Clairvaux, *Sermones de diversis.* Migne, *Patrologia Latina* 183, p. 587. Thomas à Kempis, *Imitation of Christ* II, a, 31.

5   Cf. Thomas Aquinas, *Summa Theologica* II, II, 164, 1 ad 5.

6   Johannes Pinsk, *Die sakramentale Welt*, 2nd ed. (Freiburg i. Br., 1941), p. 163.

7   See Note to the Reader, p. viii.

8   *Laws* 653 d 2.

9   Cf. Josef Pieper, *Leisure: The Basis of Culture*, rev. ed. (South Bend, Ind., 1998) pp. 3 ff.

10 Hannah Arendt, *The Human Condition* (Chicago, 1958), pp. 4 f.

11 *Phaedrus* 276 b 5.

12 *Philosophie der Weltgeschichte*, Sämtliche Werke, Jubiläumsausgabe, ed. by H. Glockner (Stuttgart, 1927–40), p. 318.

13 Cf. J. Huizinga, *Homo Ludens*, 3rd ed. (1939), p. 30.

14 Cf. Adolf Ellegaard Jensen, *Mythos und Kult bei Naturvolkern* (Wiesbaden, 1951), p. 77.

II

1   Book XI, where Augustine speaks of the concept of time.

2   *Aufzeichnungen aus den Jahren* 1875/79. Gesammelte Werke, Musarion-Ausgabe (Munich, 1922 ff.), vol. IX, p. 480.
3   Gerhard Nebel, "Die kultischen Olympien." *Frankfurter Allgemeine Zeitung* of August 20, 1960 (no. 194).
4   Martin P. Nilsson, *Griechische Feste von religiöser Bedeutung, mit Ausschluss der attischen* (Leipzig, 1906), p. 111 and p. 160.
5   Cf. Alewyn and Sälzle, *Welttheater*, p. 16.
6   Cf. Josef Pieper, *Happiness and Contemplation* (South Bend, Ind., 1998).
7   *Symposium* 212 a. Jowett's translation, modified.
8   Thomas Aquinas, *Summa contra Gentiles* 3, 37.
9   Pierre Teilhard de Chardin, *The Phenomenon of Man* (New York, Harper & Brothers, 1959), p. 31.
10 Karl Kerényi, "Vom Wesen des Festes." *Paideuma*, vol. I (Leipzig, 1938–40), p. 73.
11 Karl Kerényi, *Die antike Religion* (Amsterdam, 1940), p. 67.
12 *Commentary on the Sentences* 3 d. 37, I, 5, I and I.
13 Cf. *Reallexicon für Antike und Christentum*, vol. I (Stuttgart, 1950), col. 590.
14 Georg Wissowa, *Religion und Kultus der Römer*, 2nd ed. (Munich, 1912), p. 432.
15 *"Une offrande sacrée prise dans le temps."* C. Jullian in the article "Feriae" in *Dictionnaire des antiquités grecques et romaines*, ed. by C. Daremberg and E. Saglio (Paris, 1896), vol. II, p. 1044.
16 Kurt Eisner, *Feste der Festlosen* (Dresden, 1906).
17 Roger Caillois, "Théorie de la fête." *Nouvelle Revue Française*, vol. 53 (1939). Later included in *L'Homme et le sacré*, 3rd ed. (Paris, 1950).
18 Caillois, *L'Homme et le sacré*, p. 128.
19 Ibid., pp. 165 f.
20 Cf. Pieper, *Happiness and Contemplation*, pp. 71 f.

III

1   Chrysostom, *De sancta Pentecoste*, hom. Migne, PL 50, 455.
2   *"Ex hoc enim aliquis delectatur, quia habet bonum aliquod sibi*

conveniens vel in re vel in spe vel saltem in memoria. "
Thomas Aquinas, *Summa Theologica* I, II, 2, 6.

3 Sigisbert Kraft, "Was ist ein christliches Fest?" *Kateche-tische Blätter* no. 81 (1956), p. 6.

4 Cited in Louis de Thomassin, *Traité des festes de l'Église Traités historiques et dogmatiques,* vol. II (Paris, 1683), p. 21.

5 "Lettre à M. d'Alembert . . . *Œuvres complètes,* vol. II (Geneva, 1782), p. 386.

6 Odo Casel has rightly argued against the theory that a martyr's festival is merely a day of recollection. If the fruit of the martyrdom is not given real contemporaneity, he points out, it is difficult to see how the celebration of a martyr is to differ in principle from a Shakespeare festival. Cf. O. Casel, "Zur Idee der liturgischen Festfeier," *Jahrbuch für Liturgiewissenschaft,* vol. III (1923), p. 165.

7 J. A. Jungmann, "Das kirchliche Fest nach Idee und Grenze." Franz X. Arnold Festschrift *Verkundigung und Glaube* (Freiburg i, Br., 1958), p. 165.

8 *L'Être et le Néant* (Paris, 1943), p. 631.

9 Arthur Schopenhauer, *Aphorismen zur Lebensweisheit.* Sämtliche Werke (Insel Verlag, Leipzig), Vol. IV, p. 480.

10 *Aufzeichnungen aus den Jahren* 1880/81. Gesammelte Werke, vol. XX, p. 480.

11 *Thus Spake Zarathustra,* III (Before Sunrise). (Modern Library ed.), p. 173. This same section contains the chapter "The Seven Seals *(Or the Yea and Amen Lay)."*

12 *Nachgelassene Aufzeichnungen aus den Jahren 1882 bis 1888.* Gesammelte Werke, vol. XVI, p. 37

13 *Wille zur Macht* IV, no. 1032. Gesammelte Werke, vol. XIX, p. 352.

14 Erik Peterson, *Zeuge der Wahrheit.* Theologische Traktate (Munich, 1951), p. 203.

15 *A Kierkegaard Anthology.* Ed. by Robert Bretall (Princeton N.J., 1946), p. 351.

16 Cf. Josef Pieper, *Über die Hoffnung,* 6th ed. (Munich, 1961), pp. 58 ff.; *Leisure: The Basis of Culture,* p. 9.

17 Kierkegaard, op. cit., p. 351.

18 Cf. Kerényi, *Wesen des Festes,* pp. 64 f.

19 Paul Stengel, *Die griechischen Kultusaltertümer*, 3rd ed. (Munich, 1920), p. 191.
20 Juilian, *Feriae*, p. 1045. *"Le jour de fête n'est pas en principe, au moins chez les Romains, un jour de joie."* *Dictionnaire d'archéologie Chrétienne* V, I, col. 1403.
21 Hölderlin *Poems*, translated by Michael Hamburger (New York, 1952), p. 103.
22 Cf. Josef Pieper, "Die Verborgenheit von Hoffnung und Verzweiflung," in *Tradition als Herausforderung. Aufsätze und Reden* (Munich, 1963), pp. 165 ff.
23 Albert Camus, *The Myth of Sisyphus*, p. 123.
24 Cf. Joseph Pascher, *Eucharistia, Gestalt und Vollzug* (Münster, 1948), pp. 266 ff.
25 Thomassin, *Traité des festes*, p. 16. Origen, Contra Celsum, 8, 22.

IV

1 *Laws* 653 d 1.
2 Cf. Josef Pieper, *Über den Begriff der Tradition* (Cologne and Opladen, 1958), pp. 20 ff.
3 Jullian, *Feriae*, p. 1053.
4 For example, in the Oxford edition (vol. V, 2).
5 415 a 10.
6 Cf. *De legibus* II, 22, 55.
7 Jullian, *Feriae*, p. 1042.
8 *L'Homme et le sacré*, p. 130.
9 *Ion 535 d*.
10 Cf. P. E. Huschke, *Das alte römische Jahr und seine Tage* (Breslau, 1869), p. 233.
11 Cf. *The Festal Epistles of S. Athanasius: Translated from the Syriac*. Oxford, London, 1854.
12 *"Le sacrifice étant l'âme des Fêtes . . ."* Thomassin, Traité des festes, p. 40.
13 Hegel, *Vorlesungen über die Philosophie der Religion*. Zweiter Teil II, 2. Sämtliche Werke, vol. XVI, p. 126.
14 *Wille zur Macht* IV, no. 1052. Gesammelte Werke, Vol. XIX, p. 364.

15 Ibid, no. 916. *Gesammelte Werke*, vol. XIX, p. 292.
16 As in Apoc. 7, 12.
17 *De spiritu et littera*, 13, 22.
18 Jungmann, *Das kirchliche Fest*, p. 164.
19 A Protestant theologian has said that in truth "for man ... the seventh day is the first day of his life." (Dieter Munscheid, "Das Verständnis des Feiertages in der Bibel." *Kirche in der Zeit*, no. 12 [1957], p. 213.) Though this interpretation is somewhat forced, it does point up a real element in every holiday.
20 "... *inhérente à l'idée de fête.* " Jullian, Feriae, p. 1044.
21 Jensen, *Mythos and Kult*, p. 68.
22 Ps. 118, 24.
23 *Laws* 653 d 1; 828 a ff.
24 "*[La fête] constitue une ouverture sur le Grand Temps . . . Elle a lieu ... dans les lieux saints, qui figurent de la même façon des ouvertures sur le Grand Espace.*" Caillois, *L'Homme et le sacré*, p. 141.
25 A remark of Odo Casel, cited in Basilissa Hürtgen, "Festgestaltung aus dem Geist der Liturgie," in *Spiel und Feier*, ed. by Theodor Bogler (Maria Laach, 1955) p. 78.
26 Cf. Josef Pieper, *Enthusiasm and Divine Madness: On the Platonic Dialogue Phaedrus*. (New York, 1964.)
27 Gerhard Nebel, *Die kultischen Olympien*.
28 "Every true festival of the Lord ... is celebrated not in this eon nor on earth." Origen, *Commentary on St. John* (X, 83).
29 Although this definition is somewhat excessively psychological, it is still insufficiently "rational" to positivistic archaeologists. Ludwig Deubner, who quotes it (p. 153), calls it "too abstract" (L. Deubner, *Attische Feste*, 1932; reprinted by the Wissenschaftliche Buchgesellschaft, Darmstadt, 1956). In this same book Deubner, speaking of the festivals at which rituals of purification predominate, says that their meaning is the "cleaning of the temple" (p. 20), adding that the significance of the day as one of misfortune may be easily explained by the natural fact that in the course of such cleaning "dirt is

stirred up which fills all the air and can do damage everywhere" (p. 22). Such crude rationalizations, alas, are no help whatsoever for achieving any kind of understanding of festivals.

30 *L'Homme et le sacré*, p. 135; cf. p. 142.
31 *The Festal Epistles of S. Athanasius.*
32 Gerhard Nebel, *Die kultischen Olympien.*

V

1 Pinsk, *Sakramentale Welt*, p. 163.
2 *Georgics* 1.
3 Macrobius, *Saturnalia* I, 16, 11. Georg Wissowa has commented that just when the Roman economy began to flourish, efforts were made "by extremely involved casuistries to demonstrate that every sort of work was permissible on holidays." (*Religion und Kultus der Römer*, p. 441.)
4 *Das kirchliche Fest*, p. 166.
5 Evangelisches Soziallexikon, *ed. by F. Karrenberg* (Stuttgart, 1954); article "Sonntagsheiligung," col. 912 f.
6 Ibid.
7 I am referring principally to the controversy within Protestantism between Joachim Beckmann ("Der Feiertag in der Geschichte der Kirche") and Dieter Munscheid ("Das Verständnis des Feiertages in der Bibel") in the journal *Kirche in der Zeit* (vol. XII; 1957). Munscheid states: "Agreement on the meaning of Sunday does not exist in Protestant theology" (p. 211).
8 Karl Kerényi, *Vom Wesen des Festes*, p. 65. Friedrich Schleiermacher, in his *Praktische Theologie* (Sämtliche Werke, vol. XIII; Berlin, 1850), speaks of the "tendency of the Protestant church... to reduce festival celebrations ... to the minimum" (p. 843). And if we wish to consult the splendid, indispensable *Theologisches Wörterbuch zum Neuen Testament*, founded by Gerhart Kittel, on the subject of "Festivals," we will discover to our surprise that there is no such entry.
9 *Summa Theologica* I, II, 100, 5 ad 2.
10 *Summa Theologica* I, II, 100, 5 ad 3.

11 Basil, *De Spiritu Sancto*, cap. 27.
12 Cf. *Die Religion in Geschichte und Gegenwart (RGG)*, 3rd ed., Vol. II, col. 908.
13 Odo Casel, *Art und Sinn der ältesten christlichen Osterfeier*, p. 46.
14 C. S. Lewis, *Out of the Silent Planet* (New York, 1943), p. 76.
15 Clement of Alexandria, *Miscellanies* 7, 35, 5; cf. also 7, 49, 3.
16 Chrysostom, *De Sancta Pentecoste*, hom. I; Migne, *Patrologia Graeca* 50, 454. Similarly, *In Matthaeum*, hom. 40; Migne, *PG* 57, 437; *De fide Annae*, hom. 5; Migne, *PG* 54, 669 f.
17 Jerome, *Epistola* (ad Algasiam) 121, cap. 10; Migne, *PL* 22, 1031. Similar phraseology may be found in Tertullian (*Adversus Judaeos*, cap. 4; *Adversos Psychicos*, cap. 14). Cf. also Caesar Baronius, *Annales Ecclesiastici*, vol. I (Bar-le-Duc, 1864), pp. 488 ff.
18 Augustine, *Enarrationes in Psalmos*, 41, 9; Migne, *PL* 36, 470.
19 Cf. Schmid and Stählin, *Geschichte der griechisehen Literatur*. Erster Teil "Die klassische Période der griechischen Literatur," vol. I (Munich, 1929), p. 720, note 2.
20 *Laws* 828 b 1.
21 Otto Apelt in the Philosophische Bibliothek edition (Leipzig, 1945), p. 529.
22 Cf. Georg Wissowa, *Religion und Kultus der Romer*, p. 432, note 7.

VI

1 *Laws* 653 d 4.
2 Helmut Kuhn, *Wesen und Wirken des Kunstwerks* (Munich, 1960), p. 12.
3 Ibid.
4 *Praktische Theologie*, p. 73. "Every festival lies within the realms of art." Ibid., p. 839.
5 Gerhard Nebel, *Die kultischen Olympien*.
6 "Altern als Problem für Künstler," *Merkur*, vol. VIII (1954), p. 316.
7 Paul Höffer in the magazine *Aufbau*, 1946 vol., p. 385.
8 The phrase is Joseph de Maistre's. It is part of a sentence

whose full text is: *"La raison ne peut que parler; c'est l'amour qui chante."* Henri Bremond used it as a motto for his book *Prièra et poésie* (Paris, 1926).

9   Possibly Helmut Kuhn goes too far when he says: "Lamentation is also praise." *Wesen und Wirken des Kunstwerks*, p. 94.

10 Ibid., p. 50.

11 "Cicero, *De Oratore*, 17.

12 J. Donovan, "The Festal Origin of Human Speech." I and II. *Mind*, Old Series, vol. XVI (1891), pp. 498–506; New Series, vol. I (1892), pp. 325–391 owe the reference to this extremely important treatise to Suzanne K. Langer's *Philosophy in a New Key* (Harvard University Press, 1957), whose excellent chapter on language (pp. 103 ff.) presents similar ideas.

13 Nietzsche, *Gasammelte Werke*, vol. IX, p. 480.

14 *Aphorismen zur Lebensweisheit*, p. 480.

15 Eisner, *Feste der Festlosen*, p. 10.

16 In the introduction to his edition of the poems of the Spanish writer Jorge Guillén (Zurich, 1952), p. 8.

17 Plato in his last dialogue, *The Sophist*, particularly devoted to this subject of "sophistry," speaks of the mendacious evocation of images of reality. It is precisely that, he says, which is the art of the Sophist, whom he calls "an illusionist, an imitator of real things" (*Sophist* 234).

18 "Only, where are they? the flowers, the familiar, the crowns of the feast-day?

. . .

Why no more does a god mark a mortal man's forehead... ?

. . .

Or himself he appeared, assuming the shape of a mortal, Comforting, brought to a close, ended the heavenly feast.

But, my friend, we have come too late. True, the gods are living,
But over our heads, above in a different world.

. . .

... But meanwhile it seems to me often
Better to sleep than ...
Thus to wait, and what's to be done or said in the meantime

I do not know, and what are poets for in a period of dearth?"
(*Bread and Wine*, stanzas 6 and 7, from *Hölderlin Poems* translated by Michael Hamburger, published by Pantheon Books, New York)

VII

1 "The holy man is not sick because his sickness sickens him. Therefore he is not sick." (Lao-tzu, *Tao Tê Ching*, chap. 71.)

2 Plato, *Gorgias* 464 c-d.

3 Jullian, *Feriae*, p. 1054.

4 Cf. *Herder-Korrespondenz*, vol. XIV (1959), pp. 62 f.

5 This, of course, is not intended to suggest that a holiday can be shifted at will; and it would be ludicrous to propose that the Church should provide those workers who work on the "calendar Sunday" with "a genuine and complete 'seventh day' in the course of the week," with the divine services to be held during the week. These are to be embellished with "high-quality music" and "staffed by personalities" who "will have a faculty for exerting a powerful attraction upon the working personnel in all vocations." This proposal, whose sinister terminology outstrips a normal imagination, comes from a contribution to a discussion of "Sunday Work" (published as an editorial in the *Industrie-Kurier* of August 16, 1960).

6 Cf. on this point the excellent excursus that Theodor Schieder has included in his book, *Das deutsche Kaiserreich von 1871 als Nationalstaat* (Cologne and Opladen, 1961).

7 For the "equestrian ballet" performed on the occasion of the wedding of Leopold I at Vienna in January 1667, the director, Alessandro Carducci, was imported from Italy and received a fee of two hundred thousand gulden from the Emperor. Cf. Alewyn and Sälzle, *Das grosse Welt-theater*, p. 106.

8 Ibid., p. 79.

9 Ibid., p. 14.

10 Albert Mathiez, *Les Origines des cultes révolutionnaires* (1789–1792) (Paris, 1904), pp. 50 f.

11 Cf. N. Pisani, *L'Église de Paris at la Révolution*, 2 vols, (Paris, 1909 f.)

12 Pierre de la Gorce, *Histoire religieuse de la Révolution Française* (Paris, 1949), vol. III, pp. 50, 71.

13 Jules Renouvier, *Histoire de l'art pendant la Révolution, considérée principalement dans les estampes* (Paris, 1863), p. 424.

14 *La Moniteur* (vol. XX, pp. 653 f.). Cf. de la Gorce, *Histoire religieuse*, vol. III, p. 376.

15 Egon Friedell, *A Cultural History of the Modern Age* (New York, 1954), vol. II, p. 383.

16 Thus Camille Desmoulins in his report of the following day. Cf. David Lloyd Dowd, *Pageant-Master of the Republic: Jacques-Louis David and the French Revolution*. University of Nebraska Studies; New Series, no. 3 (1948), p. 51.

17 "... *la première fête philosophique.*" Renouvier, *Histoire de l'art*, p. 417.

18 Mathiez, *Les Origines*, p. 41.

19 *Louis David. Pièces diverses sur le rôle de cet artiste pendant la Révolution.* Nouvelles Archives de l'Art Français (Paris, 1872). Jean Vallery-Radot, "David, ordonnateur des Fêtes Révolutionnaires." *L'Art vivant*, vol. I (1925), pp. 23–27. Also the book by D. L. Dowd mentioned in Note 16.

20 De la Gorce, *Histoire religieuse*, vol. III, pp. 55 f. C. Normand, "David et la fête de la reunion." *L'Art*, vol. LVII (1894), pp. 60–73.

21 Friedell, *Cultural History*, vol. II, p. 384.

22 For example, the following proposal in 1792: The mayor is to pronounce the prayer to the Supreme Being, and then the citizens, forming in choruses, with musical accompaniment, are to sing the seventeen articles of the Declaration of the Rights of Man, while simultaneously a fire blazes up. Cf. Mathiez, *Les Origines*, p. 132. Another plan was so unfortunately phrased that the hearers burst into gales of laughter. Among the festivals which were supposed to celebrate periods in human life, someone suggested that after the Festival of Youth, Mar-

riage, and Old Age there be another which he had named "Festival of the Animals *as Companions of Man*." De la Gorce, *Histoire religieuse*, vol. III, p. 55.

23 Mathiez, *Les Origines*, pp. 47 f.

24 De la Gorce, *Histoire religieuse*, vol. III, pp. 376 ff.

25 F.-A. Aulard, *Le Culte de la raison et la culte de l'Être Suprême* (1793–1794) (Paris, 1892), p. 321.

26 Friedell, *Cultural History*, vol. II, p. 383.

27 P. J. Proudhon, who oddly enough began his literary career with an essay on the celebration of Sunday (*L'Utilité de la célébration du dimanche*), is completely right: "For one day the servants regain their human dignity and place themselves once more on a level with their masters." (Quoted from the German translation: Die *Sonntagsfeier, aus dem Gesichtspunkt des öffentlichen Gesundheitswesens, der Moral und der Familien- und bürgerlichen Verhältnisse betrachtet* [Kassel, 1850], p. 18.)

28 *Isthmian Odes* 2, 23.

29 J. Beckmann, *Der Feiertag in der Geschichte der Kirche*, p. 145.

30 Cf. David Lloyd Dowd, *Pageant-Master of the Republic*, p. 60. Jacques Louis David, explaining another project for a planned festival, similarly declared that the people were "*à la fois l'ornement et l'objet.*" Cf. Firmin-Didot, *Nouvelle biographie générale*, vol. XIII, p. 230.

31 *Lettre à M. d'Alembert*, pp. 385 f.

32 Mathiez, *Les Origines*, p. 27.

33 Ibid., p .20.

34 Ernst Jünger, *Blätter und Steine* (Hamburg, 1934), p. 175.

VIII

1 Thus Friedrich Heer, "Welt-Ostern I960," *Frankfurter Allgemeine Zeitung*, Easter edition, 1960.

2 Friedrich Giovanoli, *Die Maifeierbewegung, ihre wirtschaftlichen und soziologischen Ursprünge und Wirkungen*. Basel Dissertation (Karlsruhe, 1925), pp. 5 ff.

3 Ibid., p. 16.

4 lbid., p. 121.

5   Thus the Social Democratic Congresses of 1892 (Berlin) and 1893 (Cologne). Cf. Giovanoli, p. 17.

6   At the International Socialist Workers Congress in Zurich (1893), Cf, Giovanoli, p. 18

7   Thus a manifesto of the Italian Syndicalists (1908). Cf. Giovanoli, p. 109.

8   Giovanoli, p. 115.

9   From a "Festival Essay on the May Day Celebration"; quoted by Giovanoli, p. 101.

10 *Feste der Festlosen*, p. 21. Far more cautiously, as it were in the conditional mood, Eduard Bernstein, the "theoretician of Social Democracy," says: "If our age were still capable of creating folk festivals in the manner of the old religious holidays, I would say that May Day would certainly have to become such a folk festival." Quoted by Giovanoli, p. 115.

11 *Russische Korrespondenz*, vol. 1920, nos. 8–9 (June 1920), p. 65.

12 Ibid., p. 61.

13 Ibid., p. 62.

14 Ibid., p. 59.

15 Ibid., p. 62.

16 Ibid., p. 65.

17 Ibid., pp. 66 f.

18 Giovanoli, p. 84.

19 Alewyn and Sälzle, *Das grosse Welttheater*, p. 14.

20 F. Lora, *Der 1. Mai. Der Nationalfeiertag des deutschen Volkes Feiern für Schule und Volksgemeinschaft.* (Neuer Berliner Buchvertrieb, Berlin, 1933.)

21 Proclamation of Joseph Goebbels for May 1, 1933.

22 Hitler's speech on May Day, 1935. Cf. Gerhard Starcke (ed.), *Der Nationale Feiertag des deutschen Volkes 1933, 1934, 1935* (Berlin, 1935), p. 98.

IX

1   *L'Homme et le sacré*, p. 8.

2   *Ecce homo*, Gesammelte Werke, vol. XXI, p. 278.

3   *Gedanken und Entwürfe zu "Wir Philologen,"* Gesammelte Werke, vol. VII, p. 217.
4   *Wille zur Macht,* Gesammelte Werke, vol. XVIII, p. 22.
5   Ibid., p. 48.
6   *Ecce homo,* Gesammelte Werke, vol. XXI, p. 262.
7   Caillois, *L'Homme et le sacré,* pp. 248 f.
8   *The Phenomenon of Man* (New York, 1959), p. 229.
9   The first two phrases are those of Martin Heidegger (*An Introduction to Metaphysics,* Anchor Books, New York, 1961), p. 37. Cf. also p. 32.
10 *Stadien auf dem,* Lebensweg (Jena, 1922), p. 76.
11 Bertolt Brecht in the magnificent poem, "*An die Nachgeborenen.* "
12 Thomas Aquinas, *Quaestiones disp. de Potentia Dei* 5, 4 ad 6; *Commentary on the Sentences* 4, d. 46, 1, 3 ad 6; 2, 2, 1 ad 4.
13 "*Sicut solus Deus potest creare, ita solus Deus potest creatures in nihilum redigere.*" Thomas Aquinas, *Summa theologica* III, 13, 2. "*Creavit emin Deus ut essent omnia, ut dicitur Sap. 1, 14, non ut in nihilum cederent.*" Thomas Aquinas, *Quaestiones quodlibetales* 4, 4.
14 Kurt Eisner, *Feste der Festlosen,* p. 9.
15 Cf. Josef Pieper, "Bewirken und Bedeuten," in *Tradition als Heransforderung,* pp. 137 f.
16 Heidegger, *An Introduction to Metaphysics,* p. 37.

INDEX OF NAMES